INTRODUCING

Psychoanalysis

Ivan Ward and Oscar Zarate

Edited by Richard Appignanesi

ICON BOOKS UK   **TOTEM BOOKS USA**

Published in the United Kingdom
in 2000 by Icon Books Ltd.,
Grange Road, Duxford,
Cambridge CB2 4QF
e-mail: info@iconbooks.co.uk
www.iconbooks.co.uk

Sold in the UK, Europe, South Africa
and Asia by Faber and Faber Ltd.,
3 Queen Square, London WC1N 3AU
or their agents

Distributed in the UK, Europe,
South Africa and Asia by
Macmillan Distribution Ltd.,
Houndmills, Basingstoke RG21 6XS

Published in Australia in 2000
by Allen & Unwin Pty. Ltd.,
PO Box 8500, 83 Alexander Street,
Crows Nest, NSW 2065

Reprinted 2002

Published in the United States
in 2000 by Totem Books
Inquiries to: Icon Books Ltd.,
Grange Road, Duxford,
Cambridge CB2 4QF, UK
e-mail: info@iconbooks.co.uk
www.iconbooks.co.uk

In the United States,
distributed to the trade by
National Book Network Inc.,
4720 Boston Way, Lanham,
Maryland 20706

Distributed in Canada by
Penguin Books Canada,
10 Alcorn Avenue, Suite 300,
Toronto, Ontario M4V 3B2

ISBN 1 84046 176 4

Printed and bound in Australia
by McPherson's Printing Group, Victoria

What is Psychoanalysis?

Psychoanalysis is a theory of the human mind, a therapy for mental distress, an instrument of research, and a profession. A complex intellectual, medical and sociological phenomenon.

It was conceived in the late 1890s by the Austrian physician **Sigmund Freud** (1856–1939), who is still the figure most closely associated with the subject and most often attacked by critics.

I HAD TO PAY HEAVILY FOR THIS. PEOPLE DID NOT BELIEVE MY FACTS AND THOUGHT MY THEORIES UNSAVOURY ...

Freud was forced to leave his home in Vienna when Nazi Germany annexed Austria in 1938. He emigrated with his family to London, England, in June of that year. And it was there, at 20 Maresfield Gardens, in December 1938, less than a year before his death, that Freud broadcast a statement for the BBC. He summarized his life's work and the history of psychoanalysis.

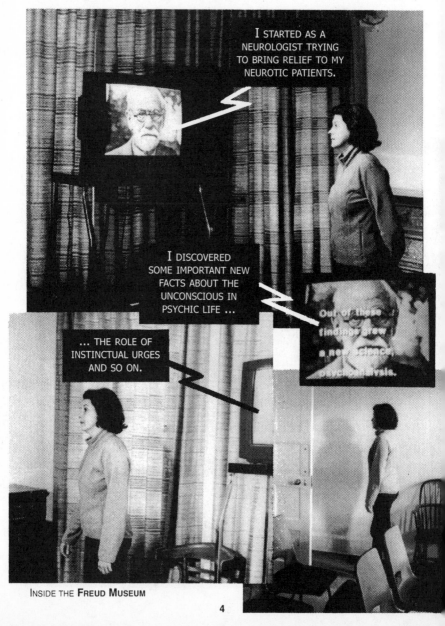

I STARTED AS A NEUROLOGIST TRYING TO BRING RELIEF TO MY NEUROTIC PATIENTS.

I DISCOVERED SOME IMPORTANT NEW FACTS ABOUT THE UNCONSCIOUS IN PSYCHIC LIFE ...

Out of these findings grew a new science: psychoanalysis.

... THE ROLE OF INSTINCTUAL URGES AND SO ON.

INSIDE THE **FREUD MUSEUM**

Today we are familiar with psychoanalysis from all the jokes and cartoon images that take some knowledge of it for granted.

Many of its concepts have become everyday cultural currency: "Freudian slip", "wish fulfilment", "Oedipus Complex", "libido", "dream symbolism", "sexual stages", "oral and anal personalities", "ego, id and superego", "repression" and the "unconscious".

Psychoanalysis is more than a particular set of concepts and therapeutic procedures. For good or ill, it has become, as W.H. Auden wrote, a "whole climate of opinion". It has given us a way to understand the "irrational" in human life as consistent with what we know of the "rational". It has elucidated the importance of sexuality in human motivation. It has shown that psychological events have hidden meanings. It has emphasized the fundamental importance of childhood. It has recognized psychic conflict and mental pain as an inescapable part of the human condition.

It can truly be said that psychoanalysis has transformed the way we see ourselves in modern "Western" societies.

A Part of Psychology

"OUT OF THESE FINDINGS GREW A NEW SCIENCE, PSYCHOANALYSIS — A PART OF PSYCHOLOGY — AND A NEW METHOD OF TREATMENT OF THE NEUROSES."

WILLIAM JAMES

JEAN PIAGET

IVAN PAVLOV

WILHELM WUNDT

CARL JUNG

Psychoanalysis is part of **psychology.** Some key psychologists are pictured with Freud. Brief sketches of their contributions can be found at the end of this book on pages 173–174, along with the psychoanalysts named in the text. For Freud, psychoanalysis is about memories, thoughts, feelings, phantasies, intentions, wishes, ideals, beliefs, psychological conflict, and all that stuff inside what we like to call our minds.

A Depth Psychology

Freud called psychoanalysis a "depth psychology" because of its assumption of an unconscious part of the mind, and because he saw it as a *comprehensive* theory.

The metaphor of "depth" implies a stratified concept of the mind, one layer laid upon another. It is often assumed that the "deeper" the level, the more "primitive" and dangerous the contents.

In this model, the analyst's role is to translate conscious thoughts, feelings, phantasies and behaviour into their unconscious antecedents (and supposed determinants). The patient says: "You've changed your curtains." The analyst says: "You're only saying that because you love your mother." Not all psychoanalysts agree with this assumption of depth.

SINCE THERE IS NO WORKABLE METHOD FOR DISCOVERING THE CONTENTS OF A PARTICULAR UNCONSCIOUS, THEN THE PSYCHOANALYST IS AT SERIOUS RISK OF SIMPLY MAKING IT ALL UP TO FIT PRECONCEIVED NOTIONS.

IT COULD BE ARGUED THAT THE UNCONSCIOUS POSTULATE HAS BECOME OUR COLLECTIVE FANTASY, A GHOST IN THE MACHINE WHICH CAN EXPLAIN ALMOST ANYTHING AND WHICH ONLY WE, THE PSYCHOANALYSTS, CAN IDENTIFY.

Donald Spence

The Dream Work

In Freud's *The Interpretation of Dreams* (1900), the metaphor of depth is reproduced in the distinction between the "manifest content" of the dream and the unconscious "latent content". Linking the two is a system of transformations – the *dream work*. Interpretation turns the strange and alien manifest dream into something with *psychical meaning* – an unconscious "wish" that the subject is attempting to express.

BUT FREUD SAYS IT IS NOT STRAIGHTFORWARD TO TRANSLATE FROM ONE LEVEL TO THE OTHER.

A DREAM NEVER TELLS US WHETHER ITS ELEMENTS ARE TO BE INTERPRETED LITERALLY OR IN A FIGURATIVE SENSE OR WHETHER THEY ARE TO BE CONNECTED TO THE MATERIAL OF THE DREAM-THOUGHTS DIRECTLY OR THROUGH THE INTERMEDIARY OF SOME INTERPOLATED PHRASEOLOGY.

"In interpreting any dream-element, it is in general doubtful..."
Whether it is to be taken in a positive or negative sense (as an antithetical relation).
If the dream element is "fire", it could stand for "water".
"Whether it is to be interpreted historically (as a recollection)."
It could be a fire you have witnessed.
"Whether it is to be interpreted symbolically"
Come on baby, light my fire.
"Or whether its interpretation is to depend on its wording."
Perhaps you would like to fire your boss.

The Search for Meaning

In other words, you just don't know. All that the psychoanalyst can do is try to gather more and more associations and see if things start to coalesce. You find yourself on a psychical spaghetti junction, with only a few bits of theory to signpost the way. Most of us would love to know what our dreams mean.

WE AVIDLY READ DREAM DICTIONARIES AND WOULD LIKE TO IMPRESS OUR FRIENDS BY INTERPRETING THEIR DREAMS.

BUT PSYCHOANALYSIS DOESN'T PROVIDE SIMPLE ANSWERS; THERE ARE MULTIPLE MEANINGS AND ENDLESS ASSOCIATIONS.

IT IS MORE TO DO WITH THE PROCESS THAN ANY FINAL "MEANING".

But, at the same time, there are a few certainties that we can hold on to. (1) Everyone dreams; (2) everyone recognizes that some of the things in dreams are connected to what has happened to us in our waking lives; and (3) everyone has some obscure notion that dreams must "mean" something.

Freud distinguished his concept of the unconscious from previous concepts. Psychoanalysis is not only a depth psychology but also a dynamic psychology, with a concept of a **dynamic unconscious**.

What is a Dynamic Unconscious?

Most people believe in a descriptive unconscious of some kind. Many of our everyday functions are unconscious – eating, walking, even talking – and life would be impossible if they were not.

When psychoanalysts talk of a "dynamic" unconscious, they add a lot more weight to the notion by their assumptions of the role that it is always playing in our lives.

IT IS CONTINUOUSLY AT WORK MOTIVATING OUR BEHAVIOUR.

THE CONTENTS OF THE UNCONSCIOUS ARE DESCRIBED AS DYNAMIC – INSTINCTUAL FORCES, WISHES, UNCONSCIOUS PHANTASIES, INTERNAL OBJECT RELATIONS.

AND WE PLACE IMPORTANCE ON CHILDHOOD EXPERIENCES AS DYNAMIC OR "MOTIVE FORCES".

Freud used the example of post-hypnotic suggestion to show the existence of the unconscious. The hypnotized person does not know why he is carrying out the suggestion made to him under hypnosis ("eat onions", "pretend to be a dog", "open your umbrella and hold it above my head", or "sing *Somewhere over the rainbow*").

ARF! ARF! ARF!

ONIONS ARE VERY GOOD FOR YOU.

HE MAKES UP ALL KINDS OF SPURIOUS REASONS TO EXPLAIN HIS CONDUCT.

I WANTED TO PRACTICE BARKING TO SCARE POTENTIAL BURGLARS.

I THOUGHT AS IT WAS RAINING YOU MIGHT LIKE TO TRY MY UMBRELLA.

THE SONG JUST POPPED INTO MY HEAD.

The unconscious influence makes him distort reality.

The Unconscious is Mysterious – not Mystical

Dreams allow us a glimpse into a different world. But the unconscious is not a mystical or occult phenomenon. It is simply a part of the mind.

A SPIRITUALIST MIGHT ASSERT THE EXISTENCE OF "SPIRIT GUIDES" LOOKING OVER ONE.

THE PSYCHOANALYST MIGHT TALK OF INTROJECTIONS OF PARENTAL FIGURES (OR ASPECTS OF THEM) INTO THE SUPEREGO.

THE OCCULTIST MIGHT TALK OF THOUGHTS COMMUNICATED FROM ANOTHER WORLD.

THE PSYCHOANALYST MIGHT SPEAK OF THE SUBTLE UNCONSCIOUS COMMUNICATION OF THE TRANSFERENCE RELATION.

Whereas the regression therapist might talk of "past lives" (e.g. Grandma says: "I love you so much I want to eat you up – I must have been a cannibal in a previous life."), the psychoanalyst might talk of the life we had before language or below the barrier of repression and infantile amnesia.

In practice, psychoanalysts use many different models to think about what's "in" the unconscious, how it is structured and how it affects behaviour. They see these contents in a dynamic sense as urges that motivate both the creative expression of the person and the inhibitions, symptoms and anxieties that may seem to deplete him of energy, tie him in knots or undermine his possibilities for enjoying life.

Joseph Sandler

I HAVE ARGUED THAT THE UNCONSCIOUS NOT ONLY CONTAINS THE SEXUAL AND AGGRESSIVE IMPULSES OF THE CHILD BUT ALSO EMBODIES EGO CAPACITIES, DEFENSIVE FUNCTIONS, CHILDHOOD THEORIES AND SO ON.

THE UNCONSCIOUS IS CONCEIVED AS A "CHILD WITHIN".

The Hidden Forces of Behaviour

Sometimes these contents may be organized mental products
(elaborate phantasies, for instance); at other times they are derivatives
of repressed drives (such as "cannibalistic" urges to "incorporate") or
unconscious body images (as full of something "bad", for instance);
they may be infantile representations of parents, or repetitions of early
patterns of relationships; they may be unconscious infantile forms of
thinking; they may be unconscious psychic functions, defence
mechanisms or psychical universals.

But it could also involve grandiose phantasies based around derivatives of micturation – just as in the story by **Rabelais** (1483–1553),Gargantua sat astride Nôtre Dame and drenched the city below.

"MY AGGRESSIVE INFANTILE URGE TO MAKE FIRES AND DESTROY THE CONTENTS OF BUILDINGS (MOTHER'S BODY) MAY HAVE BEEN TURNED ROUND INTO THE DESIRE TO PUT FIRES OUT".

"IN PUTTING FIRES OUT, I MAY BE REPRODUCING ASPECTS OF AN EARLY RELATIONSHIP, PERHAPS PLACATING A PARENT WHO MAY EXPLODE AT ANY MOMENT OR WHO THREATENS TO COLLAPSE IN FRONT OF ME".

"OR PROVING WHAT A GOOD BOY I AM BY CONTROLLING MY FIERY TEMPER".

ALL OF THESE FACTORS MIGHT CONTRIBUTE TO MY DECISION TO BE A FIREMAN - AND MIGHT BE TEASED OUT WITH A FEW YEARS' ANALYSIS!

Of course, he wouldn't bother unless things started to fall apart and being a fireman was not enough to maintain his self-esteem or psychic equilibrium. Then he might want to know how he got there, stuck up a ladder in a state of panic.

19

Psychoanalysts often feel embarrassed to talk about the unconscious in public, because it all seems so daft. Freud said that it seems like that because we have to put unconscious processes into words. If such and such an unconscious process was turned into the language of consciousness, it would be like this … For instance, small children may be afraid of falling down the toilet. But suppose an adult person is passed over for promotion and begins to feel that his life is not worth living …

Could these two mental situations be related?

Psychoanalysis would say that they could be. In the adult, there is a child fearing to be sucked down into a black hole, a terrifying void, abandoned and alone, who feels that he is losing a part of himself and that nobody cares or understands, whose bodily products (his little "jobs") are not valued, and who may secretly wish to be washed away. Now a psychoanalyst cannot prove a connection, but certain things give him clues.

And that's where the unconscious influence of the past comes in.

The Knowable Mind

Above all, "the unconscious" is a concept which is there to aid thinking. It functions as a concept to bring order to the data of analysis (what patients say in analysis) and also to the vagaries of human behaviour. We don't really know what is in the unconscious. It is a means by which we can draw inferences and explain otherwise irrational aspects of human life, and also see the hidden irrationality of normal behaviour.

THE PROBLEM OF OTHER MINDS STOPS BEING FRAGMENTED AND UNKNOWABLE.

WE START TO GET SOME GRIP ON IT, AND CAN GATHER MORE EVIDENCE TO SUPPORT OR REFUTE OUR HYPOTHESES ABOUT THE UNDERLYING CAUSES OF BEHAVIOUR.

It makes the world lawful again. In effect, it is the core belief of psychoanalysis, and the idea, for Freud, that made psychoanalysis scientific and "a part of psychology".

But could Freud be wrong? Could psychoanalysis be another kind of knowledge altogether?

Is Psychoanalysis a Religion?

Many critics see psychoanalysis as a kind of religion, with its holy texts, its hierarchies and churches, disciples spreading the good news, promises of salvation, and claims to truth.

Others see it as a secret cult out to brainwash people or bamboozle them into parting with their money.

Most psychoanalysts have a somewhat less exalted sense of Freud's power.

Shamanism and Psychoanalysis

A psychoanalyst might point out that there is a sharp opposition between psychoanalysis and any kind of fundamentalist religion based on the literal reading of religious texts. Psychoanalysis is defined by the *questioning* of the literal meanings of things – and its own "sacred texts" are continually reassessed.

But might psychoanalysis be nevertheless akin to faith healing or shamanic ritual? The anthropologist **Claude Lévi-Strauss** (b. 1908) examined a shamanic ritual from the Cuna population of Panama and drew parallels with psychoanalysis.

THE PURPOSE OF THE RITUAL IS TO FACILITATE DIFFICULT CHILDBIRTH.

IT INVOLVES THE ELABORATE RENDITION OF A MYTH BY THE SHAMAN, ENLISTING SPIRIT FORCES ONTO THE SIDE OF THE WOMAN IN HER STRUGGLE TO RESTORE HER **PURBA** OR SOUL.

The shaman's words – his rendition and enactment of the myth – reintegrate the woman's suffering within a whole cosmology where everything is meaningful, and in doing so, real changes occur. Does psychoanalysis, too, anchor people's lives in a new kind of individual mythology – of good and bad objects, Oedipal struggles, internal worlds, trauma and repression, which the patient uses to put together a fragmented psyche?

Some Crucial Differences

A psychoanalyst might smile at this "shamanic" description of her practice. Without wishing to disparage the shaman's art, or the efficacy of his interventions, she might nevertheless point out some crucial differences.

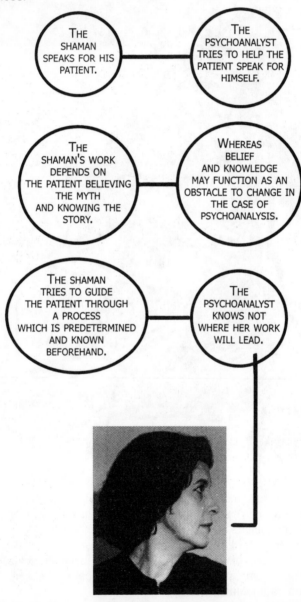

THE SHAMAN SPEAKS FOR HIS PATIENT.

THE PSYCHOANALYST TRIES TO HELP THE PATIENT SPEAK FOR HIMSELF.

THE SHAMAN'S WORK DEPENDS ON THE PATIENT BELIEVING THE MYTH AND KNOWING THE STORY.

WHEREAS BELIEF AND KNOWLEDGE MAY FUNCTION AS AN OBSTACLE TO CHANGE IN THE CASE OF PSYCHOANALYSIS.

THE SHAMAN TRIES TO GUIDE THE PATIENT THROUGH A PROCESS WHICH IS PREDETERMINED AND KNOWN BEFOREHAND.

THE PSYCHOANALYST KNOWS NOT WHERE HER WORK WILL LEAD.

A Substitute for Religion?

But is psychoanalysis a *substitute* for religion? Did the radical changes affecting 19th-century life result in a breakdown of traditional social bonds and a loss of certainty which was *replaced* by psychoanalysis? Urbanization, feminism, the rise of consumerism, industrialization, railways, telephones, Darwin, science and sexology …

WHEN NIETZSCHE DECLARED "GOD IS DEAD", DID PSYCHOANALYSIS COME IN TO FILL THE GAP AND SOLEMNLY DECLARE "GOD IS UNCONSCIOUS"?

Psychoanalysis is not a Religious Rite

Could the ideas of psychoanalysis be used to offer a kind of religious consolation to the people who have lost their faith? A new kind of community of believers; a new kind of certainty about self and identity; a new kind of morality about sin and redemption; a new kind of succour in the arms of an all-loving parent figure.

HAS THE PSYCHOANALYST TAKEN THE PLACE OF THE PRIEST? HAS THE PROCESS OF ANALYSIS TAKEN THE PLACE OF CONFESSION?

QUITE THE CONTRARY. THE PERSON WHO COMES TO ANALYSIS DOES NOT KNOW HIS "SINS". IF HE KNEW THEM, HE WOULD NOT BE IN ANALYSIS.

Nevertheless, psychoanalysis may have something in common with a "spiritual quest". But for Freud, and many subsequent psychoanalysts, *metaphysics* is not *metapsychology*. Freud committed himself to "our god Logos", Reason, and pinned his analytic colours firmly to the mast of science.

Is Psychoanalysis a Science?

We like to think that science gives certain knowledge and rests on proven "facts". It is supposed to be value-free and independent of contamination by personal or cultural prejudice. Its theories involve measurable quantities and can be proven by repeatable experiments. This naive empiricist view was not shared by Freud. He saw the relation between scientific theories, their "data" and the phenomena of reality in a more dynamic and interactive way.

"MEDIOCRE SPIRITS DEMAND OF SCIENCE A KIND OF CERTAINTY WHICH IT CANNOT GIVE, A SORT OF RELIGIOUS SATISFACTION. ONLY THE REAL, RARE, TRUE SCIENTIFIC MINDS CAN ENDURE DOUBT, WHICH IS ATTACHED TO ALL OUR KNOWLEDGE. I ALWAYS ENVY THE PHYSICISTS AND MATHEMATICIANS WHO CAN STAND ON FIRM GROUND. I HOVER, SO TO SPEAK, IN THE AIR. MENTAL EVENTS SEEM TO BE IMMEASURABLE AND PROBABLY ALWAYS WILL BE."

Freud's Metapsychology

Human development is a "chaotic" and complex process. Freud thought that every mental process had to be considered from three different angles to get a complete picture, as a physicist might look at light first as a wave and then as a particle.

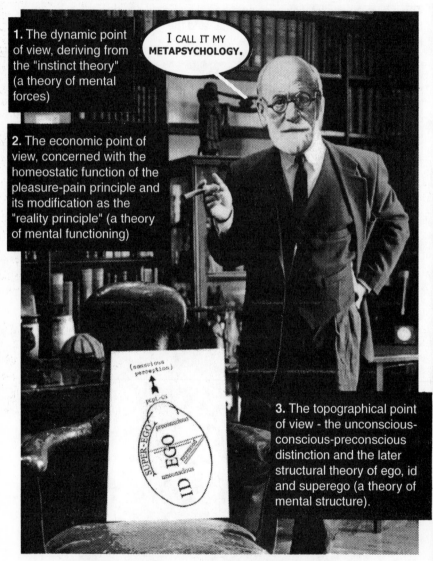

1. The dynamic point of view, deriving from the "instinct theory" (a theory of mental forces)

I CALL IT MY **METAPSYCHOLOGY.**

2. The economic point of view, concerned with the homeostatic function of the pleasure-pain principle and its modification as the "reality principle" (a theory of mental functioning)

3. The topographical point of view - the unconscious-conscious-preconscious distinction and the later structural theory of ego, id and superego (a theory of mental structure).

Think of all the factors involved when a person falls in love. It's not just "blind instinct", is it?

The complexity of mental development opens up a degree of indeterminacy which makes us feel uncomfortable with a "scientific theory". It is impossible for psychoanalysis to follow some of the usual procedures of science. It cannot perform easily repeatable experiments or make predictions about outcomes that can be explicitly stated.

WHY CAN THE OUTCOMES NOT BE PREDICTED?

FIRST, BECAUSE WE CAN NEVER KNOW EXACTLY THE INITIAL CONDITIONS OF THE SYSTEM (WHAT FREUD CALLS "THE CONSTITUTIONAL FACTOR").

SECOND, BECAUSE SO MUCH HAPPENS IN A PERSON'S LIFE THAT WILL PUSH DEVELOPMENT ONE WAY OR ANOTHER (THE "EXIGENCIES OF LIFE").

THIRD, BECAUSE OF THE MANY INTERACTIONS BETWEEN THE PARTS OF THE SYSTEM WE ARE STUDYING.

Inappropriate Scientific Proof

A psychoanalyst cannot say to a doting parent: "Yes, your child *will* be a doctor." But she could certainly say: "Yes, your child *will* have intense childhood experiences and relationships, and whatever her profession – even if she becomes a psychoanalyst – her choice will be influenced by the vicissitudes of those experiences and the reaction formations and sublimations which develop to negotiate them."

Experiments designed to "test" psychoanalytic concepts frequently strike psychoanalysts as trivial or downright funny.

One study was designed to test whether "oral passive wishes" had an important role in causing peptic ulcers. The researchers reasoned that people with "oral passive wishes" would choose bland, sweet, wet foods as opposed to seasoned, bitter or dry foods.

THE EXPERIMENT CONFIRMED THE HYPOTHESIS — UNTIL HANS EYSENCK POINTED OUT ...

SUBJECTS PREFER THESE FOODS FOR THE SIMPLE REASON THAT THEY ARE EASIER TO DIGEST.

The notion that an "oral passive wish" can be isolated and deemed to function as a cause of behaviour is bizarre. The person who eats (and loves and hates) and has appetites and tastes and food preferences, is not an isolated drive component but a whole person in relation to the world. Attempting to "prove" psychoanalytic theory in these "scientific" terms is like asking a chemist to show you the value of a ruby or a diamond.

What Sort of Science Is It?

If psychoanalysis is a science, it is the science of a complex object that cannot be adequately defined by a methodology which isolates single factors while holding the rest of the system constant. It attempts to explain the irrational in human nature by offering explanations in which the sums "add up". Where there are no supernatural or mystical forces, and the often irrational outputs of human behaviour must be accounted for by hypotheses about inputs (unconscious phantasies, urges, desires) and their origin. This attitude of wanting the world to make sense in its own terms, without the necessity for God, is perhaps what defines "science" as much as anything else.

LIKE ALL SCIENCES, IT DEVELOPS CONCEPTS APPROPRIATE TO ITS OBJECT — THE **UNCONSCIOUS** — AND IT HAS THE RIGHT TO EXPECT THESE CONCEPTS NOT TO BE CONFUSED WITH "REALITY".

Nobody asked Newton to put the concept of gravity in a bottle. It was there to explain a relation in the theory, just as, say, the concept of "libido".

Just because psychoanalytic theory is indeterminate, and "hovers, so to speak, in the air", as Freud put it, does not alter its conceptual status.

"PSYCHOANALYSIS BEGAN AS A METHOD OF TREATMENT; BUT I DO NOT WANT TO COMMEND IT TO YOUR INTEREST AS A METHOD OF TREATMENT BUT ON ACCOUNT OF THE TRUTHS IT CONTAINS, ON ACCOUNT OF THE INFORMATION IT GIVES US ABOUT WHAT CONCERNS HUMAN BEINGS MOST OF ALL — THEIR OWN NATURE — AND ON ACCOUNT OF THE CONNECTIONS IT DISCLOSES BETWEEN THE MOST DIFFERENT OF THEIR ACTIVITIES ..."

Psychoanalysis is a *species-specific psychology* (it does not apply to rats or pigeons) and Freud's impulse in creating it was not necessarily to "cure" people but to solve some of the riddles that pertain to what we might call "the human condition".

The Hermeneutic Critique

Some philosophers and psychoanalysts have argued that psychoanalysis should abandon its outmoded language of biological forces and mental structures and embrace an entirely "hermeneutic" outlook. Psychoanalysis is concerned with finding "meaning" in a patient's words or symptoms, or in cultural productions. As soon as Freud took this step, it is said, psychoanalysis became a different kind of enterprise, because meaning is not the product of causes but the creation of a human subject.

HERMENEUTICS HAS ITS ROOTS IN RELIGION.

ORIGINALLY, IT REFERRED TO THE INTERROGATION OF HOLY TEXTS TO DISCOVER THE INTRICACIES OF THE HIDDEN MESSAGE THAT THE ALMIGHTY WAS IMPARTING.

In this view, psychoanalysis becomes the equivalent of telling stories of the patient's life; or creating new stories. The patient and analyst enter a process of negotiation in which a "better" story is constructed that finds a place for what has previously been hidden, repressed or disavowed.

Telling a Better Story

What is looked for is a fit between the parts and the whole. Not scientific "proof", but a story that is coherent and consistent and that makes sense of the symptoms, behaviours and difficulties with which the patient had originally gone for help.

IT'S LIKE PUTTING TOGETHER A JIGSAW IN WHICH HALF THE PIECES ARE MISSING AND HAVE TO BE FOUND BEFORE YOU CAN COMPLETE THE PICTURE.

OR FINISHING A POEM IN WHICH HALF THE WORDS HAVE BEEN ERASED.

The analyst helps find the missing pieces by means of his "theories", or "master narratives", as the psychoanalyst **Roy Schafer** calls them, depending on the particular school that he has been trained in.

Psychoanalysis is Not Story-Telling

Whether this means that analysis can be abandoned for literary "synthesis" is not clear. For Freud, psychoanalysis was concerned not only with what a person says, but with what he *wants*, and how those wants become represented in his life. It is not just about *meaning*, but about determinate *motives* and the *mechanisms* by which these motives get expressed.

AND IT IS NOT ABOUT **CONSTRUCTING** SOMETHING, BUT **UNPICKING** SOMETHING.

But what kinds of specific ideas about human nature, the mind and its troubles have psychoanalysts come up with over the years, and what is the data to support them? It is to this question that we now turn.

Some Weird Ideas

"SUPPOSE THAT SOMEONE COMES ALONG AND ASSERTS THAT THE CORE OF THE EARTH CONSISTS OF JAM. ... WE SHALL ASK OURSELVES WHAT SORT OF PERSON THIS MUST BE WHO CAN ARRIVE AT SUCH A NOTION, OR AT MOST WE SHALL ASK HIM WHERE HE GOT IT FROM. THE UNLUCKY INVENTOR OF THE JAM THEORY WILL BE VERY MUCH INSULTED AND WILL COMPLAIN THAT WE ARE REFUSING TO MAKE AN OBJECTIVE INVESTIGATION OF HIS ASSERTION ON THE GROUND OF A PRETENDEDLY SCIENTIFIC PREJUDICE".

Are the assertions of psychoanalysis like saying that the centre of the earth is made of jam? Let's now look at some key ideas of psychoanalysis and see if it's "jam theory".

The Importance of Sexuality

Imagine you are Sigmund Freud and you ask yourself the question:

And here are the answers he came up with ...

No Mating Season

Human sexuality is quite peculiar and unique. It is not like a duck's, or a rabbit's, or a chimpanzee's. The distinguishing feature is the *loss of oestrus.*

THE **PERIODIC** CHARACTER OF SEXUAL EXCITATION DISAPPEARS, AND THE RELATION BETWEEN FEMALE MENSTRUATION AND MALE EXCITATION IS COMPLETELY TRANSFORMED.

IN OTHER WORDS, "MALE EXCITATION" IS NO LONGER DEPENDENT ON A FEMALE SEXUAL CYCLE.

SEXUALITY HAS BECOME UNHINGED FROM REPRODUCTION. HUMAN BEINGS HAVE BECOME "OBSESSED WITH SEX".

Other Peculiarities of Human Sexuality

Human sexuality is capable of ***displacement***. Freud said that we would find it odd if hunger could be satisfied by reading a menu, but with the sexual drive this is precisely what seems to happen. Sexual activity can be displaced onto non-sexual objects to become "perversions". Sexual energy can be channelled into non-sexual activities or combined with emotions such as aggression or fear.

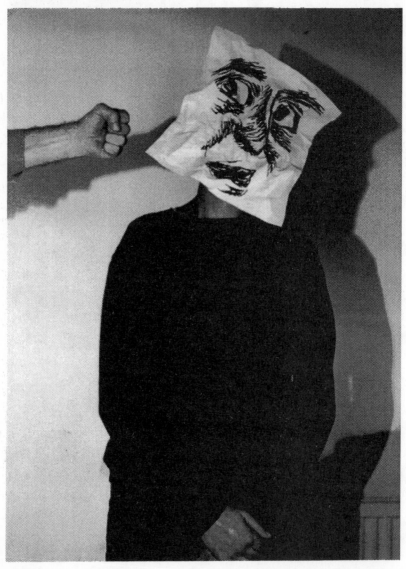

In all societies, there are **symbolic** regulations of sexuality to replace the lost biological "mating season" regulation.

IDEAS ABOUT "MALE" AND "FEMALE" IDENTITY.

AND RULES AND REGULATIONS ABOUT WHO CAN MARRY WHOM.

WHAT COUNTS AS LEGITIMATE SEXUAL BEHAVIOUR.

The most important regulation is the "incest taboo" which establishes a boundary between generations and is essential for the origin of kinship systems and social organization.

Troublesome Sexuality

Freud discovered that sexuality seemed to cause much trouble for his patients, and was often at the root of their distress. It seemed strange to think that a "natural" function could cause so much inner turmoil and psychic conflict. People got bewitched, bothered and bewildered about the whole damn business – and still do.

The French psychoanalyst **André Green** laments: "It is as if sexuality was considered a topic of specialized significance, a limited area of the internal world among others."

Childhood Sexuality

One of Freud's rhetorical tricks was to side with popular opinion against the "experts". "Every mother and nursemaid knows", he used to say, "that children play with themselves, have a lively interest in sexual matters, play 'doctors and nurses', and investigate the riddle of the difference between the sexes. The only people who don't seem to know these things are the doctors and so-called experts."

Were Freud alive today, he might point out some contradictions in our attitude to childhood sexuality.

We want children to read and write and be clever at school, yet we expect them to be ignorant as far as sexuality is concerned.

We want children to love their parents, but not to feel emotions of rivalry or jealousy that we know to be frequently associated with love.

We accept that young children have sensual bodily feelings, but we deny that they may be associated with psychological content (wishes, phantasies or ideas), or be directed to other people.

We deny sexuality to children, but strangely enough we want to assume that little boys and little girls are pre-formed. That is to say, we want to retain the main criterion of sexuality!

The result of these contradictions is that the child is left with the most innocent and rarefied "spiritual" love on the one hand, and a stupid and ineffable body on the other.

Body and Mind Connected

Psychoanalysts assume that children are less stupid than we like to imagine. The mind has a synthesizing capacity for making connections between sense data. Bodily sensations are connected to emotional states (fear, frustration, satisfaction, anger) and directed towards important people ("objects") in the outside world.

This process does not reach its adult form until well after puberty.

Sexual development is not the whole picture for psychoanalysis. The child develops as an integrated person, synthesizing an array of internal and external influences. His psychic structure, relations to other people, emotions, self control, sense of reality, gender identity, sense of right and wrong and so on are all interacting.

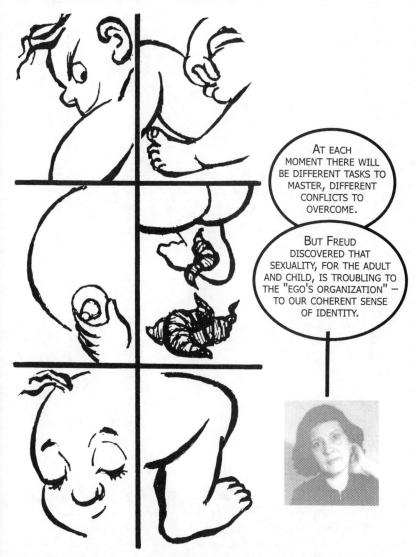

AT EACH MOMENT THERE WILL BE DIFFERENT TASKS TO MASTER, DIFFERENT CONFLICTS TO OVERCOME.

BUT FREUD DISCOVERED THAT SEXUALITY, FOR THE ADULT AND CHILD, IS TROUBLING TO THE "EGO'S ORGANIZATION" – TO OUR COHERENT SENSE OF IDENTITY.

The child's sexuality – and the sublimations, identifications and adjustments he makes to cope with it – is not the same as an adult sexuality, despite the fact that many non-genital aspects continue into adulthood.

The Abuse of Children

In his last book, *An Outline of Psychoanalysis* (1938), Freud emphasized, as he had done in his early work, the pathogenic effect of the sexual abuse of children by adults.

IMPOSING ADULT SEXUALITY INTO CHILDREN IS AN ATTACK ON THEIR INTEGRITY.

IT THREATENS THE PRECARIOUS IDENTITY THAT THE CHILD IS ESTABLISHING.

The adult who should support the child in his or her efforts to master his or her feelings, uses the child for his or her own needs. The adult who should protect, attacks the child instead. The adult who should maintain the social boundary, transgresses the boundary and undermines the capacity for trust. **Sándor Ferenczi** asserted that the trauma is not only the sexual violation but the sense of betrayal and confusion.

The Oedipus Complex

One of the troubling aspects of these early childhood sensuous-emotional relations is that our feelings come into conflict with each other. Love and jealousy, rivalry and dependence are all mixed up together, directed to parents or their substitutes. Ambivalence is the order of the day. The **Oedipus Complex** isn't a simple "love your mother and hate your father" complex (for boys).

The active side of the emotion (to "want") is opposed by the passive side (to be wanted). It is not so much a state as a process.

Placing the Oedipus Complex

For Freud, the Oedipus Complex was part of human evolution – the inevitable result of a long period of childhood dependence and the existence of an incest taboo.

Later it became virtually a definition of psychoanalysis itself: "A person's **emotional attitude** towards his family, or in the narrower sense towards his father and mother."

Freud considered the Oedipus Complex to be a universal of human nature – but each individual embodies that complex in a unique, idiosyncratic and particular way.

Emotional Attitudes

Psychoanalysts see the effects of these "emotional attitudes" to family members each day in their practice. A man may come to analysis because he is unable to form satisfactory relationships. Perhaps he is excessively "choosy" and always finds faults in potential partners. Or he is unable to bring together the dimensions of love and sexual enjoyment.

WHEN I CHOOSE LOVE, I BECOME INHIBITED IN MY SEXUALITY.

WHEN I CHOOSE SEX I BECOME EMOTIONALLY FROZEN AND SECRETLY DESPISE MY NEW PARTNER.

Analysis might help him to understand his problem in terms of the Oedipus Complex.

Unconscious Infantile Images

In analysis he may see that if he allows himself a fully engaging physical relationship with a cherished person, he is brought into rivalry with his father – or rather the *unconscious infantile image* of his father. Oscillating between love and sensuality saves him from the possibility of Oedipal rivalry – at the cost of immaturity and loneliness.

It also maintains an idealized image of his mother and projects the negative feelings that might otherwise overwhelm him. He and his partners suffer from his inability to escape from the shadow of Oedipus.

Or think how difficult it is for teenagers and many adults to tolerate the thought of their parents' intercourse. Why should that be unless the thought resonated with some deep emotional experience? **Melanie Klein** assumed that an Oedipal situation was present from a very early age.

A BABY AS YOUNG AS NINE MONTHS MAY HAVE AN OBSCURE SENSE OF A TRIANGULAR RELATIONSHIP AND A PHANTASY-SENSE OF SOMETHING "INSIDE" THE MOTHER, WHICH I DESIGNATE "THE FATHER'S PENIS".

It sounds ridiculous apart from the fact that the mother does have something inside her which affects the baby – her milk – as well as internal mental representations of the father and father substitutes.

From the baby's point of view, it may be that the mother's to-ings and fro-ings will be interpreted as her having something precious inside her that is connected to a "third term" – whether or not the father is actually present. The precious thing gives the mother a life outside the baby. Not what you want if you are that baby!

So in some ways the acknowledgment of the Oedipal situation is to acknowledge that you are not the only one.

You are forced to acknowledge a time before your own existence, and the sexual encounter that created you. Descartes was wrong when he said "I **think**, therefore I am", but it's more comforting than the alternative!

Castration Complex

Freud first wrote of the castration complex in an essay, "The Sexual Theories of Children". On one level, it is a purely empirical question to see if children come up with such ideas about sexual difference. But Freud took this children's theory and turned it into something of fundamental importance for development. Even psychoanalysts are embarrassed by the idea and relegate castration to some vague sense of powerlessness and feelings of "impotency", which may indeed be part of the story.

But there is more to penises than meets the eye. If, for instance, you laugh at a man during a sexual encounter, he will lose his erection or become aggressive.

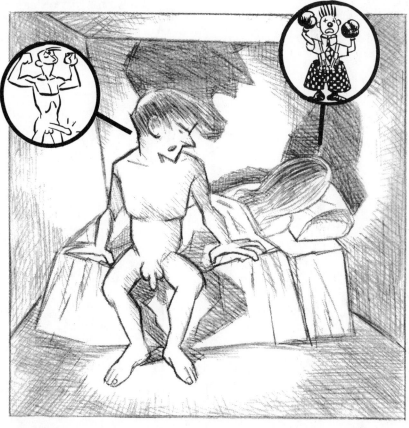

His penis is connected not just to the *sexual* function but also to preservation of his ego. His penis has meanings and "cathexes" (mental energy attached to an idea, memory or object) from many sources.

Many Levels of Meaning

Once the penis becomes the primary organ of *pleasure*, any threat to it becomes a threat to all pleasure – what **Ernest Jones** called "aphanisis". Once it becomes an object of *self-regard*, any threat to it becomes a massive blow to narcissistic integrity – losing a part of your self. Once it becomes a means of *sexual congress*, any threat to it becomes a threat to our connection with a loved one. Once it becomes associated with *procreation*, any threat to it becomes a threat to future potency.

Penis Envy

Some people consider the concept of penis envy unacceptable.
Karen Horney pointed out that Freud's schema of sexual development took the boys' point of view as the standard by which girls were evaluated, and inevitably skewed the results in a "sexist" direction. But are the elements of penis envy too ridiculous to contemplate?

IT WILL HARDLY BE NEWS TO ANY PARENT THAT CHILDREN ARE ENVIOUS OF EACH OTHER OVER NEARLY EVERY DIFFERENCE THAT DISTINGUISHES THEM.

As **Jacques Lacan** said: "Man's desire is the desire of the Other." It is not unreasonable to suppose that in the process of establishing their own identity, children will consider the problem of the difference between the sexes. Would it be so strange for them to come to the conclusion that it is the presence and absence of the penis that is the dominant characteristic?

Establishing Identity

"Penis envy" and the "castration complex" may be processes that help to stabilize identity. These are crucial moments when the option of being the other sex is closed down and the child assumes the psychological identity of a little "boy" or a little "girl". The girl starts to envy the penis, according to Freud, when she begins to realize that she does not have one and will not be able to get one in the future.

Untransformed Penis Envy

But imagine a little girl who grows up feeling that she can never do anything right because she has not got what it takes to be loved by her father.
Or a girl who lives with a gnawing sense that she has missed out on something precious in her life.
Or another who grows up feeling physically damaged in some unspecified way.

These painful situations really do exist. They arise in childhood and are connected to ideas about the body. For Freud, the concept of "penis envy" groups these phenomena in a coherent manner. It could be called the "female castration complex".

Shifting the Emphasis

Some psychoanalysts have also talked of a "womb envy" – envious and depressive feelings that boys may feel when they realize they will never be able to have a baby.

They offer other explanations, perhaps based on the baby's sense of fusion with and separation from the mother's all-powerful breast. Emphasis shifts to envy of the mother's **potency** and her **interior space**, rather than the external sign of the penis.

Whatever the case, many psychoanalytic ideas that seem so alien to our experience can be broken down into smaller elements with which we are familiar. Others are found elsewhere. Grotesque ideas are found in mythological stories, "primitive" belief systems or modern art. Weird ideas come to us in dreams. Strange theories come out of the mouths of children. Psychoanalysts do not just make it all up out of their own heads!

Models of the Mind

But if these are some weird ideas, what are the models of the mind that hold it all together?

Imagine you are a neuroscientist and could shrink yourself down to the size of a brain cell.

You find yourself in an enormous jungle of neurons, overlapping and intertwining, breaking and forming connections, switching on and off in a seemingly arbitrary fashion ...

Yet despite these chaotic, stochastic processes, you know that brains give rise to regularities and patterns, maps and consistencies; a cohesiveness to perception and awareness.

Models and Hypotheses

As you get further from the jungle of neurons, a new kind of order emerges. You begin to develop "higher level" models of brain structure and functioning which embody hypotheses about the kinds of functional unities you infer.

MODELS **OF THE MIND** HAVE A SIMILAR RELATION TO THOUGHTS AND PHANTASIES, EXPERIENCES AND EMOTIONS - THE CONTINUOUS FLUX OF "THINGS THAT COME INTO ONE'S MIND" ...

... AS **MODELS OF BRAIN FUNCTION** HAVE TO THE SEEMINGLY CHAOTIC INTERACTION OF NEURONS.

Scientific models are not just representations of real objects, like an architect's model of a house. Although they are based on underlying metaphors, they do not just picture reality but "embody hypotheses" about the phenomena under investigation.

What are models of the mind "for"? Let's look at some answers ...

1. Models of the mind indicate hypotheses about how mental stuff is organized and regulated.

Freud's famous structural model of "**ego**", "**id**" and "**superego**", regulated in accordance with the "**pleasure principle**", is a model of this kind. On one level, the model tries to express the fact that human beings are bio-socio-individuals, and the different parts may come into conflict.

On another level the model posits a particular distribution of **psychic contents**. It carries the implication that the contents of the mind are distributed within these various "agencies", have different modes of existence and are separated by some kind of mechanisms. What are these mechanisms?

Repression

The primary mechanism for Freud is "Repression", the first "defence mechanism" and the process by which the unconscious "id" is formed and maintained. Of course, the model tells us little about how the mechanisms work in detail. Freud had a complicated theory of how repression operates.

BUT WE OFTEN USE THE TERM IN A SHORTHAND WAY TO DESCRIBE A GENERAL PUSHING AWAY OF UNACCEPTABLE IDEAS (THAT CAUSE TOO MUCH CONFLICT) INTO THE UNCONSCIOUS.

Other defensive processes also help maintain the distribution of psychic contents, including perceptions. Defences are the bobbing and weaving of the mind. We ward off the unpleasure that would be caused if we acknowledged the ideas – deflecting them, turning them round, pushing them out, putting them in a box, disguising them and so on.

A never-ending process.

Defence Mechanisms

Many defences were described by **Anna Freud** in her book *The Ego and the Mechanisms of Defence*. Freud called them "dodges".

Defence and Mental Integrity

There are many other supposed processes in the mind which have been classified as "defence mechanisms" and function to distribute and regulate the thoughts, feelings and impulses in the "mind". We could say that all mental processes are "defensive" in the sense that the mental apparatus – whatever model is used – attempts to maintain its own equilibrium.

BUT THE OPERATION OF THESE SAME PROCESSES MAY ITSELF LEAD TO FRAGMENTATION AND A BREAKDOWN OF INTEGRITY.

THE STRUCTURE AND CONTENTS MAY START TO COME APART.

2. Models embody hypotheses about how the mind develops over time.

The structural model implied a developmental sequence, with the ego and superego developing out of the id, from a primary disorganized state. The new-born baby is conceived as a bundle of sensations in a chaotic whirlpool of meaningless perceptions and stimuli.

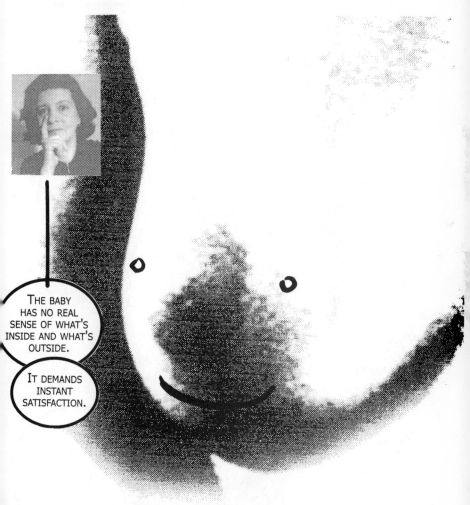

THE BABY HAS NO REAL SENSE OF WHAT'S INSIDE AND WHAT'S OUTSIDE.

IT DEMANDS INSTANT SATISFACTION.

Since there is no conception of time, any delay in having its needs met and urgent demands satisfied arouses excruciating frustration. The ego develops to modify the stimuli and organize the flux into stable and meaningful representations.

Ego Functions

The ego also localizes the generalized sensations of the body into specific bodily organs, and itself depends on the development of specific organ systems such as the visual system, myelinization of nerve fibres and so on. Thus the ego is connected both to an organization of the body – **a body ego** – and an organization of the outside world – **representations**. Over time, new forms of regulation come to the fore. The "pleasure principle" is replaced by the "reality principle" and we are able to delay gratification.

WE FIND IT ODD IF AN ADULT PERSON STARTS SCREAMING AND SHOUTING FOR HIS FOOD IN A RESTAURANT AS SOON AS THE WAITER HAS LEFT HIS TABLE.

With the growth of the superego new forms of self-regulation are established in the form of shame, guilt and self-punishment.

Psychoanalysts since Freud have questioned this developmental sequence and argue that very young babies are much more organized than the Freudian model gives them credit for. Melanie Klein suggested that an ego was present from birth and ascribed a complicated phantasy life to babies. **Margaret Mahler** spoke of the symbiosis between mother and child which gave way gradually to individuation.

Video studies of mothers and babies have demonstrated that …

... BABIES HAVE INBUILT COGNITIVE ABILITIES TO REGULATE EXPERIENCE

... RECOGNIZE OTHER PEOPLE

... AND DISTINGUISH BETWEEN THE INNER WORLD AND THE OUTER.

Babies also spend much of their lives asleep, however. "Communicating" is evidently not their only desire!

3. Models embody hypotheses about what the mind is "constructed" of.

In the "object relations" view of psychoanalysis, developed initially by **Ronald Fairbairn** and elaborated by many psychoanalysts since, the mind is not so much a psychical apparatus composed of different agencies, but an "internal world" or "theatre" in which various characters play their parts.

The object relations view rests on the assumption that human beings primarily seek relationships with other people ("objects") rather than simple "pleasure" or "discharge" of psychical tension.

"Internal objects" can be mental representations of people, or bits of people ("part objects"), or combinations of people, or even functions that people performed for you when you were little. The mind is constructed out of "internal objects".

Relations between and to the internal objects forms the basis for subsequent relationships, the outside world in general and how one feels about "oneself".

Internal Objects Dramas

Of course the internal objects are not exactly the same as the re[al]
figures they are based on. They are distorted by emotions and p[…]
The frustrating mother may turn into a witch-mother; the scolding[…]
may become a monster-father. For **John Rickman** the unconsci[ous…]
layer upon layer of such abandoned "object cathexes" – precipita[…]
early relationships and modes of functioning.

IN EACH LAYER, THE SAME OBJECTS (PARENTS, SIBLINGS AND OTHER RELATIONS) RECUR AGAIN AND AGAIN.

WITH DIFFERING DEGREES OF PRIMITIVENESS AND COMPLEXITY.

INTERACTING WITH EACH OTHER AND INFLUENCING BEHAVIOUR.

Imagine a Thanksgiving dinner – and you're the turkey!

To maintain psychic equilibrium the self tries to mould the outside world – especially other people – to fit its own patterns. As **Donald Meltzer** puts it: "The skill with which people manipulate others to play roles in the drama of their phantasy life is exceeded only by the eagerness with which people enlist to play the part prescribed."

And we enact these roles to repeat in "real life" the ancient dramas of childhood.

4. Models may embody hypotheses about how psychic contents get "into" the mind.

There is a paradox in psychoanalysis that the model of the mind that justifies the "talking cure" in Freud and Breuer's *Studies on Hysteria* (1895) is not a psychoanalytic model at all! There is no dynamic unconscious, no differentiated psychic apparatus, no instinctual life, no coherent theory of repression or psychic conflict, no real sense of psychic development and it was written before the word "psychoanalysis" was ever used.

Perhaps the person was preoccupied elsewhere; perhaps the experience overwhelmed his natural defences.

Whatever the case, it worms its way in and becomes a "foreign body", separated from the rest of the contents of the mind. And it can play tricks on the real body.

Identification

Another phenomenon of hysteria was what Freud called "hysterical identification".

In the years that followed, Freud came to regard identification as the main process by which psychic structure itself was created. Despite our best efforts, we tend to end up like our parents! Thus the superego is built up from the "residues of parents, educators and exemplars".

The growth of morality depends on the child's relation to his parents and his ability to deal with difficult internal feelings – the pre-Oedipal mother (in her "good" and "bad" aspects), ambivalence, aggression, reparation, rivalry, internalization of values, and acquisition of the rules of language.

Identifications Change

Identifications rearrange the "stuff" of our minds and change the tenor of emotions and memories.

THINGS WHICH GAVE PLEASURE IN ONE PHASE, CEASE TO GIVE PLEASURE.

THINGS WHICH WERE FEARED IN ONE PHASE, CEASE TO BRING FEAR.

THINGS WHICH WERE VALUED IN ONE PHASE, CEASE TO BE VALUED.

The whole pattern changes, like a kaleidoscope changes its configuration as you turn it.

Melanie Klein also asserted that we may **introject** qualities of other people into the ego.

AS IF WE WERE MAGICALLY EATING THEM UP AND INCORPORATING THEM INTO OUR OWN STRUCTURE.

More than half a century later, **Donald Winnicott** was also much concerned about the problem of inside and outside.

I PROPOSE THE CONCEPTS OF "TRANSITIONAL OBJECT" AND A "TRANSITIONAL SPACE" BETWEEN THE MOTHER AND CHILD.

In Winnicott's model (his way of looking at things rather than a diagrammatic model), the internal world is built up out of the interactions with a "good enough mother".

Winnicott's Dyad

There is no such thing as a baby. There is only a mother-baby dyad. We have to understand not just internal and external objects but their **mutual interaction**.

On the basis of these experiences the baby develops a core sense of security – a "true self" – that is, the basis on which the inevitable frustrations and disillusionments of life can be managed, and the real world acknowledged.

IF A CORE IDENTITY DOES NOT DEVELOP, THE CHILD, AND LATER ADULT, MAY BE UNABLE TO UNITE HIS INNER AND OUTER WORLD.

HE WILL LACK SPONTANEITY AND CAN ONLY IDENTIFY WITH **SOCIAL ROLES** RATHER THAN EXPRESS HIS INNER QUALITIES.

I PLAY AT BEING MYSELF.

Transitional Space

For Winnicott, the "transitional space" between the internal world and "reality" becomes a space for creative play and imagination.

5. Models embody hypotheses about how things get pushed out of the mind.

Melanie Klein's model of the mind emphasized the concepts of "splitting" and "projection" as fundamental processes by which psychic structure is built up and psychic equilibrium maintained. The baby's mind tries to "master stimuli". One of the ways to do that is to take the **good stuff** inside you and get rid of the bad stuff.

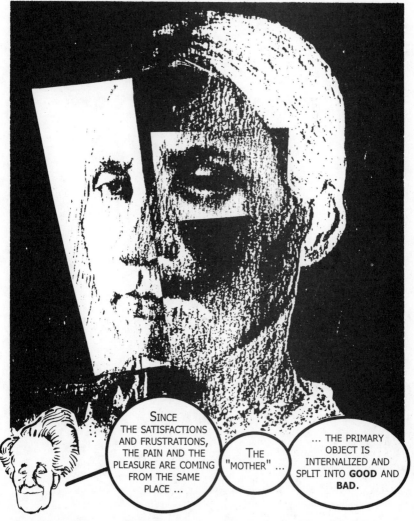

SINCE THE SATISFACTIONS AND FRUSTRATIONS, THE PAIN AND THE PLEASURE ARE COMING FROM THE SAME PLACE ...

THE "MOTHER" ...

... THE PRIMARY OBJECT IS INTERNALIZED AND SPLIT INTO **GOOD** AND **BAD.**

Psychic equilibrium is maintained by strenuously expelling the "bad" bits as well as all the rage and ferocity and frustrations they engender.

rly Phantasies of Good and Bad

ese earliest instinctual tensions in babyhood are associated with
ncrete phantasies.

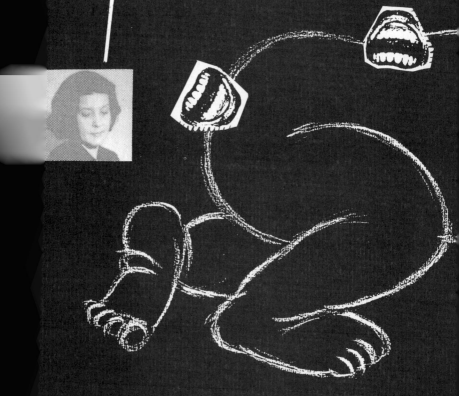

THE BABY'S HUNGER, FOR INSTANCE, IS "EXPERIENCED" (IF THAT'S THE RIGHT WORD) AS A HOSTILE PERSECUTOR ATTACKING THE TUMMY.

OR TEETHING PAINS MAY GIVE RISE TO PHANTASIES OF RIPPING APART, TEARING AND DEVOURING.

This may seem somewhat bizarre, yet it rests on a very simple
assumption that bodily sensations are interpreted by the baby, just
as pre-scientific societies (such as Lévi-Strauss's shaman) interpret
the bodily changes of illness in a concrete way by a plethora of spirits
and monsters.

The phantasy is a kind of primitive interpretation of the baby's reality, with "good" and "bad" objects causing pleasurable or unpleasurable sensations.

"BAD" THINGS ARE EJECTED FROM THE MIND, PERSECUTORS ATTACKED, AND MY OWN RAGE DEFENDED AGAINST.

AS THE BABY DEVELOPS AND CAN WITHSTAND FRUSTRATION AND DELAY WITHOUT FEARING ITS OWN ANNIHILATION, IT IS ABLE TO BRING THE GOOD AND BAD SIDES TOGETHER.

It can eventually integrate the mind and make "reparations" for the attacks on the mother. It moves from the "paranoid-schizoid" position to the "depressive" position.

Different Models Can Agree

In some sense Klein's model (which came first) is the opposite of Winnicott's.

What is Projection?

Psychoanalysts use the term **projection** to describe how people externalize the contents, or structures or relations of the internal world. We may project moods and affects, like Hamlet seeing the world "flat, stale and unprofitable" because of his own misery.

Manifold Projections

We may project aggressive feelings which come back to haunt us as malevolent "spirits". We may project needs and dependencies.

90

We may project fears, frustrations or bad experiences; the child who is told off may be seen the next moment taking control of the experience and giving her doll a similar scolding.

We may even project "structural conditions of the mind". In the children's series *Thomas the Tank Engine*, the figures of Thomas, the Fat Controller and the unruly Trucks are surely representations of the conflicts between ego, superego and id as the child experiences it?

Projective Identification

We also project into other people. Melanie Klein called it "projective identification". We put our phantasies **into** someone else, where they change that person **for us**. We might want to control the other person, or acquire their attributes, or communicate with them, by placing a bit of "ourselves" in them. It sounds strange, but we do it all the time. We suddenly feel anxious about going to a party.

IS IT BECAUSE NATALIE PHONED UP TO REMIND ME THAT PETER WAS GOING?

WHAT IS NATALIE'S PHANTASY?

IS SHE A RIVAL IN LOVE?

And in projecting that phantasy, has she actually turned you into a rival *for her*?

Or we go to watch our son play football. Go on Johnny!
But something about our tone of voice or the urgency with which we
offer encouragement makes Johnny feel judged and under scrutiny.
He starts to feel uncomfortable on the ball and make mistakes.

Have we turned Johnny into ourselves as children, buckling under the
weight of our father's criticism and expectations? Or the recipient of our
childhood phantasies of revenge?

Containment of Experience

Things from our minds get put into other people all the time. The psychoanalyst **Wilfred Bion** said that for babies it is absolutely vital that someone is there to allow that to happen. Bion suggested that the baby's and infant's projected feelings – pain, fear of death, envy, aggression – are "contained" by the mother, "detoxified" and returned to the child.

IN SOME ANIMALS, THE MOTHER PARTLY DIGESTS THE FOOD BEFORE FEEDING IT TO THE INFANT.

IN HUMAN BEINGS, THE MOTHER PARTLY DIGESTS THE EMOTIONAL EXPERIENCE WHICH THE BABY IS NOT ABLE TO ASSIMILATE ON ITS OWN.

Once again, it may seem strange. But think about how a toddler trips over and then looks to its mother before deciding whether to cry or not.

In being "looked after" the child feels relief that his emotional experience is being "understood".
In this way, the containing function is vital for the integration of the child's emerging personality.

Imagine, if you will, what life would be like if you were not understood.

EVERY TIME YOU TRY TO COMMUNICATE, THE MESSAGE GOES INTO A BLACK HOLE AND NEVER COMES BACK.

OR YOUR EFFORTS AT COMMUNICATION ARE MET WITH REJECTION.

WE CAN SEE WHY "BEING UNDERSTOOD" HAS SUCH A POWERFUL EMOTIONAL EFFECT AND RESONANCE.

Dreams, stories or art may all "contain" disturbing psychical elements, just as the mother originally did. Think about "Hansel and Gretel", or "The Three Little Pigs", or Picasso's "Guernica".

6. Models enable us to think of how psychological events are "caused", in a way that makes psychological sense.

Mental events are "overdetermined" – they have **multiple causes** – but Freud developed a "psychoanalytic" notion of causality:

"PSYCHOANALYSIS WARNS US TO ABANDON THE UNFRUITFUL ANTITHESIS OF EXTERNAL AND INTERNAL FACTORS, OF FATE AND CONSTITUTION, AND HAS TAUGHT US REGULARLY TO DISCOVER THE CAUSE OF AN OUTBREAK OF NEUROSIS IN A DEFINITE MENTAL SITUATION, WHICH CAN BE BROUGHT INTO BEING IN DIFFERENT WAYS."

We cannot read off the effect of a trauma, for instance, by looking at the precipitating external "cause". It is the interaction with the inner world which creates the "definite mental situation" and will determine the effect of the traumatic event.

OUR PETRIFIED FIREMAN AT THE TOP OF HIS LADDER MAY HAVE BEEN CRITICIZED BY A SUPERIOR, ABANDONED BY A SPOUSE, OR SLIPPED ON A BANANA SKIN AND BEEN LAUGHED AT BY COLLEAGUES.

Why Do I Do That?

If I wanted to explain why I wash my hands a hundred times a day, or cannot leave the house without checking the gas time and again, it would make little sense to follow the firing of individual neurons, or even the chains of associations and memories that I might bring up in a psychoanalytic session. What is needed is a way to organize the masses of material so it embodies appropriate causal relations.

Psychoanalytic theories have posited three fundamental causes to psychological phenomena: "experiences", "instincts" and "anxiety", and conflicts between them. More proximate causes are "wishes", "phantasies", "needs", "desires", "affects" and so on. Every "cause" can be an effect, and every effect can be a cause. Even when we appear at our most "driven" and single-minded, there are always many sources which motivate our behaviour.

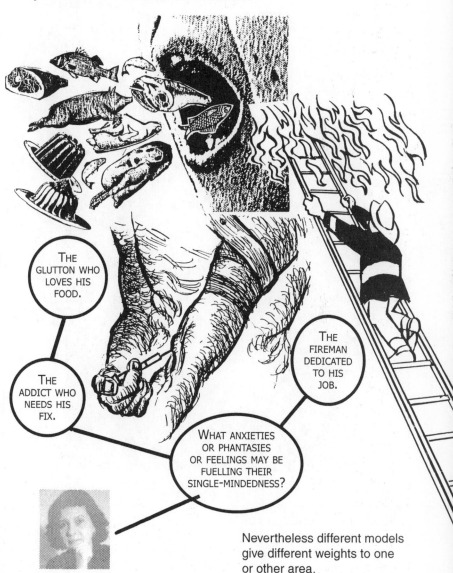

THE GLUTTON WHO LOVES HIS FOOD.

THE ADDICT WHO NEEDS HIS FIX.

THE FIREMAN DEDICATED TO HIS JOB.

WHAT ANXIETIES OR PHANTASIES OR FEELINGS MAY BE FUELLING THEIR SINGLE-MINDEDNESS?

Nevertheless different models give different weights to one or other area.

Traumatic Causes

In the trauma model, "cause" is assigned to the outside world – traumatic experiences. The trauma "causes" the symptom like a virus causes 'flu. After *Studies on Hysteria*, Freud became more interested in looking at **childhood** as the place for "ultimate causes". Ultimately, Freud decided, the "causes" of hysteria …

"… OCCUR IN THE PATIENTS' EARLIEST CHILDHOOD AND ARE TO BE DESCRIBED AS SEXUAL ABUSES IN THE NARROWEST SENSE".

The hysterical symptoms are "mnemonic symbols" of the sexual experiences. Like a virus which lies dormant for years before producing an illness. As Freud puts it: "The traumas of childhood operate in a deferred fashion as though they were fresh experiences; but they do so unconsciously." Puberty reawakens the earlier experiences like ghosts from the past that have come back to haunt us.

Separation and Attachment

Some post-Freudian psychoanalytic ideas also assign great importance to external "causes". The psychiatrist and psychoanalyst **John Bowlby** looked at the effect of separation on young children.

SEPARATION ANXIETY AND ITS EFFECTS

CLINGING BEHAVIOUR

CONSTANT WORRIES

PANIC ATTACKS

ANGER

DEPRESSION AND FEELINGS OF HOPELESSNESS

ARE RESPONSES TO REAL TRAUMATIC SEPARATIONS AND LOSSES AT CRITICAL TIMES IN CHILDHOOD.

His theory of"attachment" is based on a concept of instinct derived from **Harry S. Harlow**'s experiments in the 1950s.

Harlow's Experiment

Harlow showed that Rhesus monkeys would cling to a surrogate "terry cloth mother" rather than a wire mesh mother which provided food.

THERE IS AN INSTINCTUAL NEED FOR CONTACT WITH THE MOTHER INDEPENDENT OF HER ROLE IN SATISFYING OTHER BIOLOGICAL NEEDS.

The implication is that the quality of interaction – eye contact, fondling, engagement with the child – may be more important for developing intimacy and security than the satisfaction of basic drives. Bowlby's colleagues showed that different forms of attachment – "secure", "ambivalent" or "avoidant" – resulted in different developmental outcomes and kinds of defences.

Compromise Formation

At the same time as the childhood-trauma theory of hysteria, Freud had a more dynamic theory of obsessional neurosis which included the ideas of "repression" and "defence". The symptom becomes a "compromise formation" between the repressing forces and the repressed ideas that are repudiated by the ego. This accounts for the formation of obsessional neurosis.

"OBSESSIONAL IDEAS ARE INVARIABLY TRANSFORMED **SELF-REPROACHES** WHICH HAVE RE-EMERGED FROM REPRESSION AND WHICH ALWAYS RELATE TO SOME SEXUAL ACT THAT WAS PERFORMED WITH PLEASURE IN CHILDHOOD!"

SUCH AS INFANTILE MASTURBATION.

The memory is reactivated and the obsessional person feels he "can't trust himself" or, rather, his impulses.

Obsessional Rituals

The obsessional neurotic might have feelings of shame, or hypochondria, or fear of being noticed or being punished. He may construct obsessional rituals which act as protective measures against the obsessional memories: elaborate rituals before going to bed, or getting dressed, for instance.

The symptoms are "caused" in this case not just by the retrospective effect of the original trauma, but by the way the subject deals with it. External "cause" is changing to internal "motives". An explicit notion of psychic conflict comes to the fore.

Anxiety

In 1926, anxiety – mental pain – came to lie at the heart of psychoanalytic theory. In his work *Inhibitions, Symptoms, and Anxiety*, Freud created a developmental history of the subject that became a history of transformations in the threats which structure subjectivity. It was precisely these threats or anxiety situations – of annihilation, separation, loss of love, castration, death – that pinned the various "developmental phases" of the human being onto his or her subjectivit

IN OTHER WORDS, ANXIETY BECOMES THE CEMENT THAT JOINS THE SUBJECT TO HIS BODY.

It became the signal that set in train the defensive manoeuvres of t mind; the pain that we try to avoid but is necessary for developmen the pain that can tear us apart.

The Key Concept of Anxiety

Kleinian theorists elaborated the anxieties of persecution, of loss, and confusion (in which the actual capacity to think is threatened). Attachment theorists investigated the dynamics of separation anxiety. Anxiety became the key concept of motivation and the measure by which the mind achieves equilibrium. Even an "optimistic" psychoanalyst like Donald Winnicott, who emphasized the creative aspects of human behaviour, could say …

WHEREAS IT IS EASY TO SEE THAT CHILDREN PLAY FOR PLEASURE, IT IS MUCH MORE DIFFICULT FOR PEOPLE TO SEE THAT CHILDREN PLAY TO MASTER ANXIETY …

… OR TO MASTER IDEAS AND IMPULSES THAT LEAD TO ANXIETY IF THEY ARE NOT IN CONTROL.

7. Finally, models of the mind enable us to think about "what people are like".

Freud's essay, "The Dissection of the Psychical Personality", has led to confusion in the English-speaking world about psychoanalytic theories of "personality". Freud's essay would have been better translated as "The Dissection of the *Psychical Apparatus*", since it concerns the universal features of the "mind" according to the structural model. For a psychoanalytic theory of "personality types" – how one group of people differ from another group – we have to turn to Freud's theories of "character".

BUT WHAT WE EXPECT FROM A PSYCHOANALYTIC THEORY OF PERSONALITY IS A "GENETIC" THEORY, THAT IS TO SAY, A **DEVELOPMENTAL** ONE.

A theory which offers hypotheses about **how** these personalities come into being. Thus the first attempts at creating theories of personality were based on the "dynamic" part of the metapsychology – Freud's "instinct theory".

Freud's Instinct Theory

"INSTINCTS UNDERGO A LENGTHY PROCESS OF DEVELOPMENT BEFORE THEY ARE ALLOWED TO BECOME ACTIVE IN THE ADULT HUMAN BEING. THEY ARE INHIBITED, DIRECTED TOWARD OTHER AIMS AND DEPARTMENTS, BECOME COMMINGLED, ALTER THEIR OBJECTS, AND ARE TO SOME EXTENT TURNED BACK UPON THEIR POSSESSOR. REACTION-FORMATIONS AGAINST CERTAIN INSTINCTS TAKE THE DECEPTIVE FORM OF A CHANGE IN CONTENT, AS THOUGH EGOISM HAD CHANGED INTO ALTRUISM, OR CRUELTY INTO PITY".

"THE TRANSFORMATION OF INSTINCTS IS BROUGHT ABOUT BY TWO CO-OPERATING FACTORS, AN INTERNAL AND AN EXTERNAL. THE INTERNAL FACTOR CONSISTS IN AN INFLUENCE BY THE HUMAN NEED FOR LOVE, TAKEN IN ITS WIDEST SENSE. WE LEARN TO VALUE BEING LOVED AS AN ADVANTAGE FOR WHICH WE ARE WILLING TO SACRIFICE OTHER ADVANTAGES. THE EXTERNAL FACTOR IS THE FORCE EXERCISED BY UPBRINGING, WHICH ADVOCATES THE CLAIMS OF OUR CULTURAL ENVIRONMENT".

"IT IS NOT UNTIL ALL THESE 'VICISSITUDES TO WHICH THE INSTINCTS ARE SUBJECT' HAVE BEEN SURMOUNTED THAT WHAT WE CALL THE CHARACTER OF A HUMAN BEING IS FORMED".

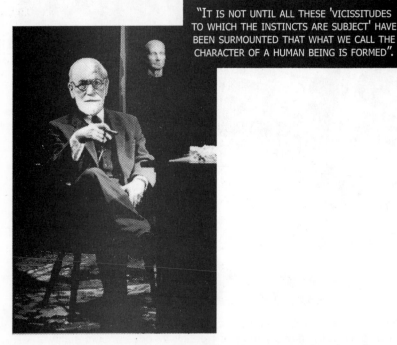

The person who overeats, for example, or is rude to waiters in restaurants, is not simply satisfying a primitive instinct for food or social status!

Phases of Development

Freud developed this approach into theories of "character" related to specific instinctual/drive constellations. As is well-known, Freud pictures a number of "component instincts", or partial drives, organized into several "phases of development" – the **oral**, **anal**, and **genital**.

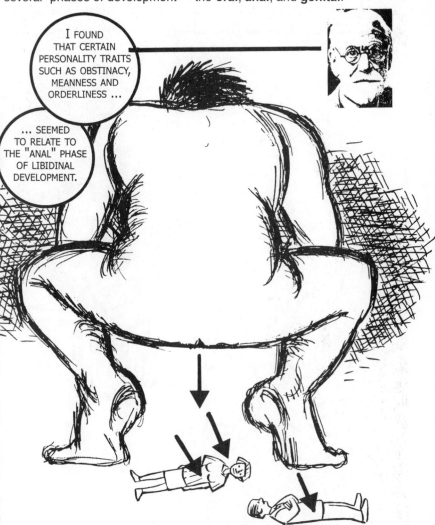

I FOUND THAT CERTAIN PERSONALITY TRAITS SUCH AS OBSTINACY, MEANNESS AND ORDERLINESS ...

... SEEMED TO RELATE TO THE "ANAL" PHASE OF LIBIDINAL DEVELOPMENT.

The bodily feelings associated with defecation were connected to mental ideas such as "destroying" or "pushing away" or "giving" or "holding on" to something; and these were connected to the primary objects in the toddler's life.

The Libidinal Subject

The mental constellation which included a **bodily experience**, **phantasy**, and a primary **relationship** formed a kind of template for the personality. Evacuation and retention, preservation and destruction, the need to control, became the dominant metaphors which moulded the developing personality and became fixed in the anal character.

SIMILARLY, WE CAN SEE THE MANY WAYS IN WHICH THE ORAL DRIVE CAN BE MANIFESTED ...

FOR INSTANCE, IN SUCKING, BITING, INGESTING, SPITTING OUT OR REFUSAL.

These can serve as templates or basic metaphors for the subject's personality as a whole and his relationships to others.

Character Armour

We meet people who are "tight-lipped" or "tight-arsed" all the time don't we? **Wilhelm Reich** coined the term "character armour" to describe the very resistant aspects of personality which have to be dealt with in analysis.

IT IS NOT JUST THE CONFIGURATION OF THE DRIVES THEMSELVES WHICH **MAKE** CHARACTER, BUT THE SYSTEMS OF DEFENCES WHICH ARE ORGANIZED TO **CONTROL** THEM.

Most people find it hard to recognize how powerful and interesting Freud's drive-based personality theory is. It is often ridiculed as asserting that personality depends on whether you were breast fed or what kind of potty training you had. Rather, it is an attempt to describe definite "mental situations", however they come about, with the qualities of a developmental "gestalt" or formation.

The Primary Self

But we could be barking up the wrong tree. Could it be the case that "personality" is the primary and superordinate structure and the drives and wants are *precipitates* of the person? This was the view of the American psychoanalyst **Heinz Kohut**. He argued that the primary entity was the "self" and that psychological functioning aimed at maintenance or restoration of the self.

PSYCHIC CONFLICT IS NOT PRIMARY BUT AN EFFECT OF **DEVELOPMENTAL DEFICITS** ...

... FAILURES IN EMPATHIC "MIRRORING", BLOWS TO SELF-ESTEEM ...

... SUCH "DEFICITS" CAN LIBERATE PERVERSE DRIVE ELEMENTS, FOR INSTANCE, AND EXACERBATED PSYCHICAL TENSIONS SUCH AS BETWEEN EGO AND IDEALS.

Healthy Narcissism

Drives, rage, perversions and so on were the products of **self-fragmentation** brought on by repeated ruptures in the patient's ties to parental figures in childhood.

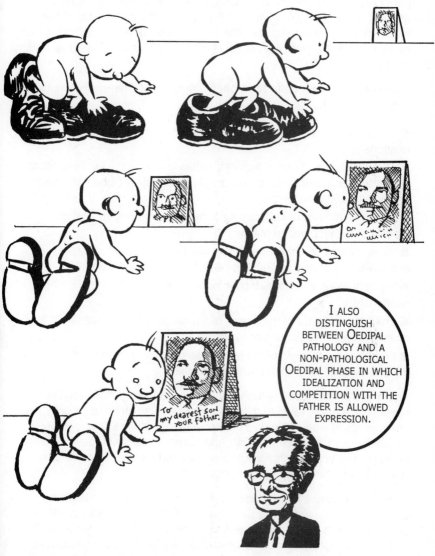

I ALSO DISTINGUISH BETWEEN OEDIPAL PATHOLOGY AND A NON-PATHOLOGICAL OEDIPAL PHASE IN WHICH IDEALIZATION AND COMPETITION WITH THE FATHER IS ALLOWED EXPRESSION.

A "mature" personality is thus based on a healthy and necessary narcissism, while developmental failures will lead to conflict and fragmentation.

A Note on Models

Models don't just fall out of the sky. They are related to the data of investigation (from patients, everyday life, literary and cultural products), to basic postulates of the discipline, to therapeutic practice, to general principles of what counts as an appropriate theory in your field of enquiry, to other people's models, and even to the personality of the model maker. A pessimist may have a model of "psychic conflict", which becomes in the hands of an optimist a model of "psychic balance" and harmony.

Since Freud's death there have been a number of changes of emphasis in model-building.

■ Concentration on the individual has given way to an emphasis on relationships.

■ The idea of the "psychic apparatus" has given way to the concept of an "inner world" with a more fluid amalgam of objects, phantasies and urges motivating the person.

■ "Conflict" models of neurosis have been augmented by "deficit" models of developmental failure.

■ An emphasis on libidinal relations has been augmented by the important role of aggression and destructiveness in development.

■"Instinctual aims" for satisfaction now include aims to form relationships.

■ The "development of the libido" has given way in some cases to the development of narcissism or the "self".

■ Emphasis on the role of the father has given way to concentration on the pre-Oedipal relationship with the mother

These are all changes in emphasis, rather than an epistemological break. Much post-Freudian theory can be seen as attempts to unify the three points of view of Freud's metapsychology. Klein's developmental "positions" and "internal objects"; Anna Freud's theory of "developmental lines"; Kohut's "psychology of the self"; and Lacan's theory of the "subject" may all be seen as attempts of this kind.

One of the reasons for producing psychoanalytic models has also changed. Freud wanted to solve some of the riddles of "human nature". With the growth of the psychoanalytic profession, the emphasis has shifted onto producing models which are useful for therapeutic practice.

It remains for the future to decide whether the pragmatic approach is the right one for psychoanalysis. Whatever the case, it should be remembered that even Freud knew that human beings have mothers and are involved in "relationships" – the Oedipal concept is a relationship theory *par excellence* – while the most "interpersonal" psychoanalyst will have an idea of internal motivating factors and psychic conflict. Those who concentrate on the subject's "real relationships" to the exclusion of phantasy and the internal world have of course abandoned psychoanalysis as a "science of the unconscious".

Although psychoanalysis may have developed different schools with their different "master narratives", there is much in common in their attempts to understand the unconscious and relieve the distress of patients. Working theories are different from models of the mind, and the practice of analysis is a very individual thing. But how does it work?

How Does Psychoanalysis Work?

From a theoretical point of view, psychoanalysis begins with the creation of a "dynamic unconscious" in *The Interpretation of Dreams*. From a therapeutic point of view it begins with the notions of "repression" and "resistance" and the "fundamental rule" of analysis: **"Say anything that comes into your mind."**

THIS TOOK PSYCHOANALYSIS AWAY FROM THE "SYMPTOM" TO AN EXAMINATION OF THE PATIENT'S LIFE AS A WHOLE.

PSYCHOANALYSIS IS THE "TALKING CURE".

It is distinguished from *psychiatry* because it does not use drugs. It is distinguished from other forms of *psychotherapy* because of the importance it attaches to free association and everything that follows from it.

But what do people go into analysis for? What are they complaining of and what did they complain of in the past? And how does analysis help to make them "better"?

Diagnosis: a Problem of Naming?

Psychoanalysts are caught in a contradiction. On the one hand, they find themselves in a medical profession, with standard clinical procedures and diagnostic categories. This was especially true in the United States, where, until recently, all psychoanalysts required medical qualifications and psychoanalysis was the dominant paradigm in psychiatry for many decades. Psychoanalysts need to pigeon-hole people as much as anyone else. They assess and categorize patients to give them a handle on the clinical situation.

IF THEY KNOW SOMEONE HAS AN "OBSESSIONAL NEUROSIS" OR "DEPRESSION", IT IS LIKE AN ASTROLOGER WHO KNOWS WHAT STAR SIGN YOU ARE.

THINGS FALL INTO PLACE. YOU KNOW WHAT TO DO.

The Anti-Diagnostic Factor

For the patient with depression, for instance, you will be able to produce a check list of basic therapeutic strategies.

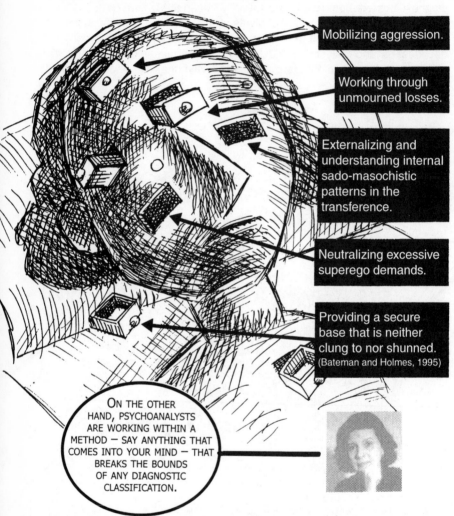

Mobilizing aggression.

Working through unmourned losses.

Externalizing and understanding internal sado-masochistic patterns in the transference.

Neutralizing excessive superego demands.

Providing a secure base that is neither clung to nor shunned. (Bateman and Holmes, 1995)

ON THE OTHER HAND, PSYCHOANALYSTS ARE WORKING WITHIN A METHOD — SAY ANYTHING THAT COMES INTO YOUR MIND — THAT BREAKS THE BOUNDS OF ANY DIAGNOSTIC CLASSIFICATION.

They are also working with a model of the mind in which things can be laid one on top of the other. Within the category of "depression", articulated around the traumatic significance of personal loss, ambivalence and guilt, may be aspects more usually associated with "obsessional neurosis" or "paranoia" or "hysteria". The analyst has to try **not** to see something – not to see the patient as an "example" of the diagnostic category. Rather, he has to develop a "psychoanalytic" orientation to the patient.

The Essence of Analysis

There are some invariant aspects of the psychoanalytic situation which the psychoanalyst must always bear in mind. Wilfred Bion advocated a notion of the "ultimate reality" of analysis: "An absolute essence which I wish to postulate as a universal quality of phenomena such as "panic", "anxiety", "fear", "love". In brief, I use "O" to represent this central feature of every situation that the psychoanalyst has to meet. With this he must be as one; with the evolution of this he must identify so that he can formulate it as an interpretation."

Let's take the latter approach!

Reasons for Analysis

People go into analysis because ...

It's Not Only Private

In all these cases we have listed – and more – the element of psychic pain is at the core of the reason for analysis.

PATIENTS MAY BE SEEN IN PRIVATE PRACTICE, IN PSYCHIATRIC CLINICS AND HOSPITALS.

OR IN SPECIAL PSYCHOANALYTIC CLINICS SUCH AS THE ANNA FREUD CENTRE OR THE TAVISTOCK CLINIC.

WHY?

WHERE?

PATIENTS MAY BE SELF-REFERRED OR REFERRED BY THEIR GENERAL PRACTICE DOCTORS.

Psychoanalysts are understandably upset when their work is denigrated as a form of "self indulgence", when they consider that the patients who see them may have been stuck in the same painful condition for years before going into psychoanalysis or psychoanalytic psychotherapy.

Another set of reasons for considering analysis are ...

But once you have decided on analysis, have found a psychoanalyst you think you can "work" with, have established the number of sessions a week (psychoanalysis is usually three or more times a week, psychoanalytic psychotherapy three sessions or less) and the cost, what happens then?

Free Association or "Freeing Something"

There are two iconic images of the practising psychoanalyst: either the silent analyst who says "Um... er..." and an occasional "That's interesting..."; or the analyst who gives you a good talking to, like a headmaster with a cowering student.

Freud called his work "analysis" because it involved breaking things down. It is an analogy from chemistry, you analyse a substance and break it down into its components.

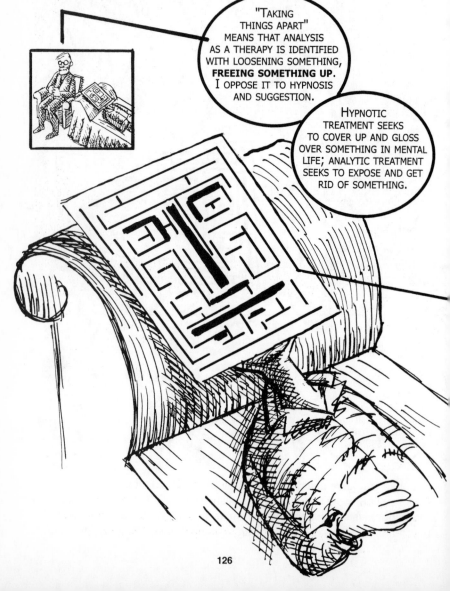

"TAKING THINGS APART" MEANS THAT ANALYSIS AS A THERAPY IS IDENTIFIED WITH LOOSENING SOMETHING, **FREEING SOMETHING UP.** I OPPOSE IT TO HYPNOSIS AND SUGGESTION.

HYPNOTIC TREATMENT SEEKS TO COVER UP AND GLOSS OVER SOMETHING IN MENTAL LIFE; ANALYTIC TREATMENT SEEKS TO EXPOSE AND GET RID OF SOMETHING.

Catharsis or Remembering

In the therapy Freud was trying to get rid of something. He tried "catharsis" at first – helping his patients remember the feelings they had at the time of the original trauma and thus exorcizing it from their minds.

And most people couldn't remember the "first time" in any case. Later on, Freud said it was as if the fire brigade went to a burning house and contented themselves with removing a lamp that had fallen over.

Making the Unconscious Conscious

Freud realized he couldn't cure symptoms in one fell swoop that had built up over years. The symptoms were like a tangled knot, with different causes from the past and present. With free association, Freud asked his patients to lie on the couch, relax, and simply say everything that came into their mind, no matter how silly or trivial or embarrassing it might seem. There was a method behind his idea.

IF I LISTEN CAREFULLY ENOUGH TO WHAT THE PERSON IS SAYING ...

... I CAN BEGIN TO SEE PATTERNS THAT REFLECT SOMETHING ABOUT HIS OR HER CHILDHOOD EXPERIENCE AND THE **MENTAL SITUATION** THAT IS DETERMINING THE ADULT NEUROSIS.

Freud's idea was that the unconscious could be made conscious, and thereby lose some of its power to distort reality and undermine the patient's mental health.

Whether he knew it or not, Freud's rule is impossible to follow. Say everything that comes into your mind? Show me the sound of one hand clapping!

THE ANALYST LISTENS NOT JUST TO WHAT THE PATIENT SAYS, BUT TO THE **HESITATIONS, REPETITIONS** AND **DEVIATIONS** THAT OCCUR AS HE TRIES TO FOLLOW THE RULE.

Analytic Listening

The analytic situation is structured within three hermeneutic horizons or temporal parameters.

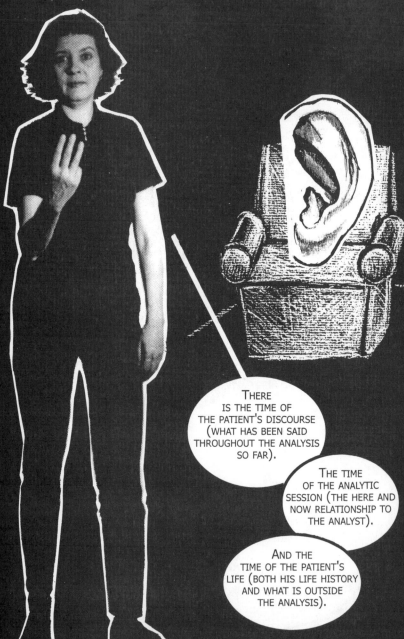

THERE IS THE TIME OF THE PATIENT'S DISCOURSE (WHAT HAS BEEN SAID THROUGHOUT THE ANALYSIS SO FAR).

THE TIME OF THE ANALYTIC SESSION (THE HERE AND NOW RELATIONSHIP TO THE ANALYST).

AND THE TIME OF THE PATIENT'S LIFE (BOTH HIS LIFE HISTORY AND WHAT IS OUTSIDE THE ANALYSIS).

The analyst tries to be attentive to all these modalities at once.

THE ANALYST HAS TO POSITION HIMSELF "EQUIDISTANT" BETWEEN EGO, ID AND SUPEREGO.

ANNA FREUD

FRED PINE

THE ANALYST MUST LISTEN TO THE DIMENSIONS OF "DRIVE", "EGO", "OBJECT" AND "SELF", AND FRAME HIS COMMENTS ACCORDINGLY.

THE ANALYST MUST LISTEN WITH THE QUESTION AT THE BACK OF HIS MIND, "HE SAYS THIS, BUT WHAT DOES HE WANT?".

JACQUES LACAN

Analytic listening involves what Freud called "evenly hovering attention", a state of reverie or meditation that allows the mind to be aware of more than one dimension at once. It is not easy. If you want to have a go, try watching an advert on TV while being aware that it is not only trying to **tell** you something (a story) but also trying to **sell** you something. The advert is coming at you from more than one level.

Listening with Indifference

This "evenly hovering attention" must also refuse to make one thing more important than another. In real life this is nearly impossible to do. If someone says "you've changed your curtains", we take this as having a different order of importance to saying that someone has died. But the analyst may simply hear "curtains" – and a resonance *at all levels* of the patient's life of traumatic changes and fears.

ANALYTIC LISTENING IS A MEANS TO AVOID "SUGGESTION".

THE ANALYST LISTENS "WITHOUT MEMORY AND DESIRE" – WITHOUT PREJUDGING THE MATERIAL.

He listens with "indifference" as Freud once called it. What can be worse than to have an analyst who is *eager to know* all your secrets? At the same time the analyst listens with interest and engagement. She is on the patient's side.

But ultimately it is impossible. In fact her own views will inevitably intrude on the situation: what she has learned from her training (in which "the teacher's error may become the pupil's dogma", as **Edward Glover** put it); her moral standards and outlook on the world.

ANALYST AND PATIENT ARE CAUGHT BETWEEN TWO IMPOSSIBLE INJUNCTIONS: "LISTEN WITHOUT MEMORY AND DESIRE" ...

... AND "SAY EVERYTHING THAT COMES INTO YOUR MIND".

BETWEEN THESE TWO IMPOSSIBILITIES THEY TRY TO FIND EACH OTHER AS HUMAN BEINGS.

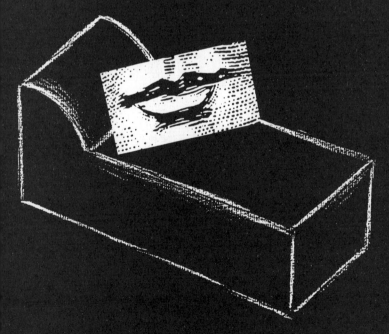

Freud called it "the impossible profession" and he meant it seriously. In fact, "failing the patient" may be part of the therapeutic effect of analysis. The analyst plays at being God, which is what the patient wants, but she has to become a person. In the process, the patient finds himself.

Aims of Psychoanalysis

No matter how thoroughgoing an analysis is, it can never grasp the "whole person". People often fear that psychoanalysis will somehow take away their individuality – their "soul", if you like. But as Freud said: "Don't worry, your friends will still recognize you". A corollary of this is that no matter how much time and thought an analyst has put in with a patient, another colleague may see things in the material that he has missed.

You could say that psychoanalysis is about "getting to know yourself better" and becoming more tolerant of the bits that are not so "nice", or "clever", or "good". "Having a better knowledge of oneself and the world is no guarantee of happiness and success, but it leads to a fuller use of potentialities external and internal" (Hanna Segal).

Psychoanalysts believe that a lot of the things people do is an attempt at flight – to run away from bits of themselves they cannot face. Often at the start of analysis a patient may have a dream that he is looking down at himself from above, or from a long way off.

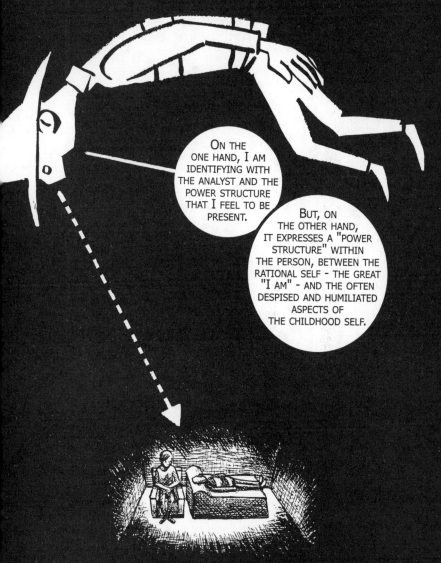

ON THE ONE HAND, I AM IDENTIFYING WITH THE ANALYST AND THE POWER STRUCTURE THAT I FEEL TO BE PRESENT.

BUT, ON THE OTHER HAND, IT EXPRESSES A "POWER STRUCTURE" WITHIN THE PERSON, BETWEEN THE RATIONAL SELF - THE GREAT "I AM" - AND THE OFTEN DESPISED AND HUMILIATED ASPECTS OF THE CHILDHOOD SELF.

By coming to terms with these childhood parts (that is, wishes, intentions, feelings that the "me" bit does not want to acknowledge), the patient begins to change.

The Process of Change

Sometimes this involves sudden insights ("Ah ha!"), sometimes it is a more gradual process, akin to growing up. Things that were important before seem to lose their meaning, tasks which had seemed difficult appear easier, relationships become less conflictual, attitudes change, life gets more interesting. Some analysts believe they offer their patients a "corrective emotional experience" to replace earlier developmental failures in their lives.

INCONSISTENCY MAY BE REPLACED BY CONSISTENCY, REJECTION BY ACCEPTANCE AND SO ON.

KLEINIAN ANALYSTS BELIEVE THAT THE FRIGHTENING IMPULSES, ALIEN ELEMENTS OR "BAD" BITS OF THE PATIENT ARE PROJECTED OUTSIDE AND DISTORT HIS PICTURE OF THE WORLD.

THE ANALYTIC TASK IS TO HELP HIM TAKE BACK THE PROJECTIONS, OVERCOME ANXIETY, AND RECONCILE THE CURRENTS OF LOVE AND HATE IN HIS LIFE.

In all cases the analyst tries to offer herself as an object that the patient can use for his own cure, as a good teacher offers herself for her students to learn.

The Problem of Resistance

But it is not so easy in practice. You know how, with some people, whenever you try to raise a particular topic of conversation, they change the subject? With others you get the feeling that there are certain subjects that are definitely taboo. Psychoanalysts get this feeling all the time.

WE ASSUME THAT THE TOPICS ARE AVOIDED BECAUSE TO CONSIDER THEM CAUSES ANXIETY. THIS IS THE BASIS FOR THE SENSE OF "RESISTANCE" THAT THE ANALYST FEELS HE IS WORKING AGAINST.

The pathogenic memories, wishes and phantasies are repressed and alienated from the conscious part of the mind – the "me" part. The work of analysis is to undo, in a sense, the alienation.

Resistance and Secondary Gain

But any particular symptom has many different causes – they are **over-determined** – and it is difficult to take apart all the elements involved. Freud also discovered that the patient did not necessarily want to get better, because there was a "secondary gain" from the illness.

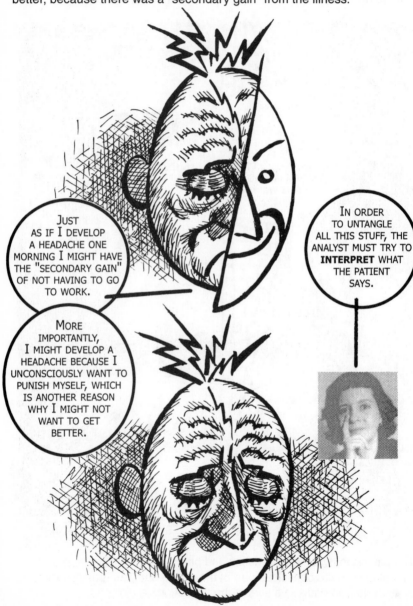

JUST AS IF I DEVELOP A HEADACHE ONE MORNING I MIGHT HAVE THE "SECONDARY GAIN" OF NOT HAVING TO GO TO WORK.

MORE IMPORTANTLY, I MIGHT DEVELOP A HEADACHE BECAUSE I UNCONSCIOUSLY WANT TO PUNISH MYSELF, WHICH IS ANOTHER REASON WHY I MIGHT NOT WANT TO GET BETTER.

IN ORDER TO UNTANGLE ALL THIS STUFF, THE ANALYST MUST TRY TO **INTERPRET** WHAT THE PATIENT SAYS.

Interpretation

Interpretation is something that we all do all the time. For instance, if we see someone running along the street, we might think that the person is running because they want to catch a bus.

They interpret what we say according to our underlying intention. But they could be completely wrong. Perhaps you just wanted to pay them a compliment! Sometimes we interpret other people's behaviour in order to get them to change. All human beings try to work out other people's behaviour and change it – usually for their own benefit.

Interpretations in Analysis

There are many different sorts of interpretations that psychoanalysts use when they are seeing patients. Here are some of the most important ones.

(1) Interpretations that relate to the patient's childhood.

PERHAPS CLIMBING THE LADDER TO THE FIRE WAS LIKE CLIMBING THAT TREE TO IMPRESS YOUR FATHER WHEN YOU WERE EIGHT.

(2) Interpretations that relate to other statements said by the patient.

YOU SAY YOU FELT EXHAUSTED WHEN YOU REACHED THE TOP OF THE LADDER.

WAS THAT LIKE THE EXHAUSTION YOU COMPLAINED OF IN YOUR SESSION ON MONDAY?

Mutative Interpretations

In framing an interpretation the analyst is trying to get hold of the unconscious wants of the patient – the urges, impulses, desires that motivate him – and use himself as a medium to fix them and make them visible. Just as a physicist sees the paths of charged particles in a cloud chamber, so the myriad traces of the patient's desires reveal themselves in analysis as they condense around the person of the analyst.

James Strachey called interpretations which achieved this aim, "mutative" interpretations.

Interpretations are used for a variety of reasons. To elicit more material and memories from the patient. To reveal a conflict, desire, or pattern of relating which is not conscious to the patient. To provide some relief for the patient by making him feel "understood" and cared for (this happens automatically when the patient has the conviction that the interpretation is "true"). To draw together various strands of therapeutic work that are being carried out.

As you can see, interpretations can both *elicit anxiety* and try to *contain* it.

The Dance of Interpretation

A crucial kind of intervention from the analyst is one that shifts the perspective of the whole situation. The patient is happily going along one track; the analyst shifts to another line. This is possible because what may be "fearful" in one register in the mind, may be "pleasurable" in another register. What is "sad" in one dimension may be a source of great rejoicing somewhere else.

As the analysis progresses, the analyst can offer more in the way of interventions that do not "understand" the patient and provide relief, but **CONFRONT** the patient and offer a different way of looking at things.

For instance, suppose the patient criticizes the analyst for being inexperienced. The analyst may detect an anxiety on the part of the patient that she will not be able to understand him.

But instead of trying to reassure the patient, or showing him that she understands and sympathizes with his fears, she might shift the focus.

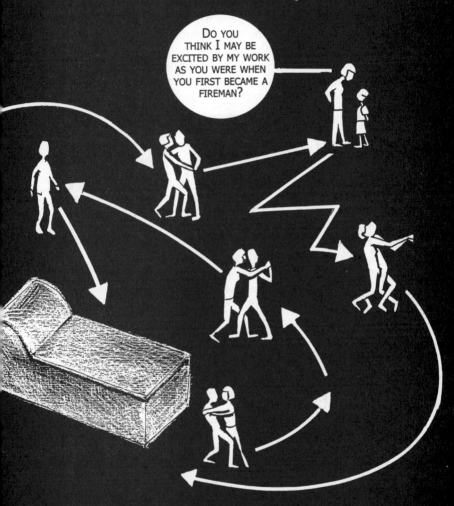

She elicits other aspects of the theme of "experience" and "inexperience". Part of the analytic process can be called an "emotional-cognitive" therapy. The result is a kind of "dance" of interpretation. The patient sees things one way and tries to push the analyst into his view of the world. The analyst pulls the patient over to another position, and the process starts again. There is an elastic thread between the two which is stretched but not broken. A framework of negotiation. Analysts often use the term "analysand" instead of "patient", to emphasize the collaborative nature of the process.

The Analytic Relationship

The difference between analytic and everyday interpretations is that the analyst tries to interpret for the benefit of the patient, rather than herself. She makes her interpretations mindful of the relation to the past life of the patient. The therapeutic hope is that with the help of another person offering support, recognition and analytic understanding, the patient will be able to work through his neurotic conflict and, as Freud once put it, "transform neurotic misery into common unhappiness".

UNFORTUNATELY, INTERPRETATIONS ARE NOT THE END OF THE STORY.

INTERPRETATIONS ARE NOT LIKE PILLS THAT A DOCTOR MIGHT GIVE TO "CLEAR SOMETHING UP".

Analysis depends on timing, intonation, inflection, empathy, the subtle nuances of intersubjective communication. All these interpretations take place within the analytic *relationship*.

I FOUND THAT THIS RELATIONSHIP BECAME A SIGNIFICANT FACTOR FOR THE PATIENT AND FOR THE PROGRESS OF THE ANALYSIS.

We must remember that a "patient" goes to a therapist because he is in some kind of difficulty which involves an element of mental pain.

What Would Your Friend Do?

Let us imagine that instead of going to a psychotherapist, the patient went on a regular basis to a friend for help in managing his mental distress, as some critics of psychotherapy have recommended. The friend might first of all try to offer advice.

If this does not seem to help, he might try other tactics.

He might listen to what the "patient" is telling him and realize that his difficulties are actually bound up with his personality as a whole. He might begin to notice that his friend is confused and does not really know what he wants.

Through these interpretations, the friend is creating implicit **theories** about the structure of the mind – that it has more than one level, for instance, or that some thoughts are less accessible to consciousness.

The Transference Problem

It might happen that within this ongoing relationship the patient talks about his past. The patient begins to look forward to seeing his friend, although sometimes he feels angry and resentful. Why does the friend seem to have everything, while the patient is so unhappy and has nothing to live for? One day the patient becomes angry for no particular reason. He shouts abuse at his friend, who is taken aback. But then the friend remembers …

The friend has realized what Freud discovered many years ago – that something about the relationship to the analyst repeats aspects of the childhood relationship – an intense, dependent, loving and hating relationship *to the parents*. It is this which provides the emotional force for the progress of the analysis and the influence of the analyst.

Freud called this factor **transference**.

And although it is evident in all relationships, it is particularly heightened in the analytic situation where the patient and analyst are prohibited from acting on their impulses in the usual way.

The analyst presents, to some extent, a blank "screen" on which the patient can project his own internal "movie" (phantasy life). In fact, before the patient enters into analysis, there is a view of "the analyst". The patient goes into analysis seeking help from *somebody*.

Four Metaphors for Transference

Transference as a battle or siege.

Transference as repetition of earlier prototypical relationships.

Transference as love – as love directed to knowledge.

Transference as a "theatre" or "intermediary realm" allowing creative work and "play".

Problems of Countertransference

The analyst finds herself playing various roles which the patient has assigned her. This function may come into conflict with her task of interpretation, in which she is forced to assert her own existence as the analyst. It is also quite difficult because the analyst too has feelings and ideas and emotional responses elicited in the analytic relationship which she has to control for the service of the analysis. The analyst does not just say whatever comes into *her* head, because what she knows and what the patient knows are two different things.

I TRY TO USE MY OWN FEELINGS AS DATA WHICH PROVIDES CLUES ABOUT THE RELATIONSHIP WITH THE PATIENT.

Yet, she too wants a "good patient", one whose progress enhances her self-esteem, or who confirms her theories and view of the world.

Subtle "behaviourist" elements may creep into the analytic encounter, a subliminal pattern of rewards and punishments influencing the direction of the treatment.

THUS THE ANALYST'S **COUNTERTRANSFERENCE** MAY PICK SOMETHING UP FROM THE PATIENT OR IMPOSE SOMETHING UPON HIM.

THE ANALYTIC COMMUNITY TRIES TO GUARD AGAINST THE LATTER BY THE LENGTHY ANALYTIC TRAINING, SUPERVISION, AND CONTINUAL DISCUSSION WITH COLLEAGUES.

The analyst's interpretations, then, are often about the analytic relationship itself. And part of the analytic process consists of freeing the patient from dependence on the analyst. The hope is that the patient will be able to live an independent, enjoyable and productive life in the future.

Is Analysis Suitable for Everyone?

Although psychoanalysts often see patients who are debilitated by their neurosis, psychoanalysis is usually regarded as a suitable treatment only for people who are "more or less" healthy. Hence the importance of assessment interviews before starting treatment. Freud did not think it was suitable for "psychoses" or people with organic brain defects.

IN PSYCHOSES, SUCH AS SCHIZOPHRENIA AND PARANOIA, THE PERSON'S RELATION TO REALITY IS DISTURBED, AND PERHAPS RECONSTITUTED IN A DELUSIONAL WAY.

BOTH CATEGORIES WERE DEEMED TO BE INCAPABLE OF FORMING A TRANSFERENCE RELATIONSHIP.

Other analysts since have tried to extend the range of patients for psychoanalysis with varying degrees of success. **Harry Stack Sullivan** worked with schizophrenic patients and developed "interpersonal" theory.

The treatment of so-called "borderline" patients (severely disturbed patients who seem to lie between psychosis and neurosis, with poor impulse control and a very distorted picture of reality) is a major part of contemporary psychoanalysis.

Recently some therapists have worked with Alzheimer's patients.

Psychoanalysts are taking on older patients, who (bizarrely) were considered too set in their ways to be able to change.

Even Freud advocated that sometimes other forms of treatment should be incorporated within psychoanalysis. He said, for instance, that patients with phobias should be brought to a point where they can confront their fears in a direct way – a behaviourist technique in his work. It might be added that Freud's "pleasure-unpleasure" principle shows he thought that in a limited aspect of our functioning, human beings follow a behaviourist logic of rewards and punishments.

Does It Work?

Much controversy still surrounds the issue of whether psychoanalysis and the other kinds of psychotherapy based on its premises actually work. A famous study by Hans Eysenck, still much cited, argued that patients in psychoanalysis improved no more than untreated controls. Subsequent studies have refuted these claims (see Holmes and Bateman 1995).

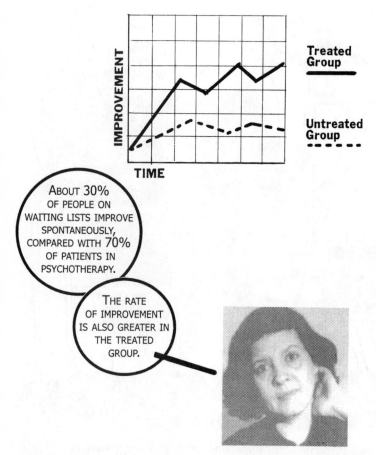

ABOUT 30% OF PEOPLE ON WAITING LISTS IMPROVE SPONTANEOUSLY, COMPARED WITH 70% OF PATIENTS IN PSYCHOTHERAPY.

THE RATE OF IMPROVEMENT IS ALSO GREATER IN THE TREATED GROUP.

Much effort is currently being put into research projects to study the effectiveness of different kinds of treatment, and this interest is not new. In one early study from the Berlin Psychoanalytic Institute, which pioneered free treatments for the poor, 60 per cent of neurotic and 20 per cent of psychotic patients were judged to have received substantial benefit from psychoanalytic psychotherapy.

It has been argued that the efficacy of psychotherapy lies in its essentially "supportive" aspects – listening to the patient, "being there" for him, showing empathy, providing a space to get things off your chest, intellectual guidance, help in dealing with life situations – rather than any specifically "psychoanalytic" aspects such as interpretation.

It is hardly surprising that psychotherapy has a therapeutic effect.

ALL PARENTS KNOW THEY INFLUENCE THEIR CHILDREN BY WHAT THEY SAY, EVEN IF THE PRECISE EFFECT OF EACH UTTERANCE IS DIFFICULT TO ASSESS.

ALL COMEDIANS KNOW THEY CAN INFLUENCE AN AUDIENCE AND RELEASE LAUGHTER WITH PROFOUND EFFECT ON FEELINGS OF WELL-BEING.

AND PSYCHOANALYSTS KNOW THAT THEY CAN FREE BLOCKAGES IN THEIR PATIENTS AND HELP THEM LIVE MORE FULFILLING LIVES.

Pyschoanalysis or Psychotherapy?

It has not been established that major differences exist between treatment outcomes for psychoanalysis and less intensive forms of psychotherapy, with fewer sessions per week and shorter duration of treatment. Psychoanalysis is the paradigm psychotherapy but it can go on for five days a week for many years.

A psychoanalyst might say that a patient's "spontaneous" recovery does not just come out of thin air; it's not spontaneous generation. It shows that there is a certain amount of "psychical work" going on, an internal therapeutic process.

The concept of "work" is fundamental to psychoanalysis. The psycho-analyst and the patient have to decide whether they can "work together". The process of achieving therapeutic change is called "working through". The psychoanalyst **Paula Heimann** called the nightly process of dreaming (the "dream-work") a *spontaneous therapy*, and also the play of humour and joking (Freud's "joke-work"), or creativity.

It could be said that "*spontaneous recovery*" is a confirmation of psychoanalytic therapy, rather than a refutation of it!
Psychoanalytic therapy is not a big mystery. It uses propensities and capabilities that are available to everyone.

The Influences of Psychoanalysis

But psychoanalysis is more than a therapy. As a science of the unconscious, it is pertinent to all aspects of human reality in which the unconscious plays a part. And it has influenced the 20th century deeply as an idea, a theory and a practice.

Psychoanalysis has applied itself to the study of the most varied aspects of **cultural life**.

FROM FAIRY STORIES TO HOUSING PROBLEMS IN SOWETO; FROM FOOTBALL TO THE NUCLEAR BOMB ...

There are four kinds of influence, direct and indirect, which psychoanalysis has had on the cultural life of modern societies.

Childcare and Education

There is a direct influence on practices such as childrearing and education. In childcare, the emphasis has shifted from "controlling" and "moulding" children, to "nurturing" and "facilitating" their development within safe "boundaries". In education, teachers may come to realize that the quality of the relationship with their pupils is just as important as the content of lessons for influencing their eagerness to learn.

CHILD PSYCHOTHERAPISTS HAVE SHOWN THAT INHIBITIONS IN LEARNING MIGHT BE AN EFFECT OF EMOTIONAL DIFFICULTIES AT HOME, OR UNDERLYING ANXIETIES ...

In fact it is a testament to the cultural changes that have taken place in the last fifty years that Ernest Jones' statement now sounds like a well-worn cliché: "Love is as necessary for a child's mental development as food is for its bodily development."

Psychoanalysis and Advertising

There is also a direct influence in practices which have tried to manipulate people – the "hidden persuaders" of advertising and public relations who use ideas about unconscious processes to organize their campaigns. Freud's brother-in-law Edward Bernays ran a successful campaign in the 1920s to get more women to smoke cigarettes.

I'VE LINKED IT TO THE QUESTION OF FREEDOM AND WOMEN'S RIGHTS. CLEVER, DON'T YOU THINK?

SO LONG AS THE FEMINISTS DON'T BLAME ME FOR THAT TOO!

Psychoanalysis and Feminism

Second, there is an indirect influence on social movements. Feminism has had an ambivalent relationship with psychoanalysis. On the one hand psychoanalysis seemed "phallo-centric", regarding women as somehow inferior to men; on the other hand many women were at the forefront of the profession. Modern feminist thinkers such as **Julia Kristeva** and **Juliet Mitchell** have themselves become psychoanalysts. Some feminists have argued that Freud minimized evidence of sexual abuse and put it all down to phantasy; others say he was the first doctor who truly listened to his patients.

WOMEN UNITE!
TALK ABOUT WHAT WE CAN DO
DO WHAT WE TALK ABOUT

child care
education
peace in our
parish

FEMINISM

CONGRESS TO UNITE WOMEN

THE WOMEN'S LIBERATION MOVEMENT

PSYCHOANALYSIS SEEMED TO DISCOUNT THE SOCIAL CONDITIONS OF WOMEN ...

BUT IT PROVIDED A UNIQUE WAY TO THINK ABOUT THE STRUCTURE OF PATRIARCHY OR THE SUBJECTIVE EXPERIENCE OF BEING A WOMAN.

It has been seen as a truly liberating theory, or as the apotheosis of male dominance – getting inside your head and twisting it around.

Pyschoanalysis and Anti-Racism

Similarly psychoanalysis has been influential in the study of racism and anti-racist education.

THE DEMONS OF THE RACIST IMAGINATION - SEX AND DIRT, SAVAGERY AND IGNORANCE - HAVE ROOTS IN THE UNCONSCIOUS AS WELL AS SOCIETY.

The processes of scapegoating, envy, aversion and denigration have been analysed. "Institutional racism" operates "unconsciously".

Psychoanalysis, Ecology and Politics

Psychoanalytic ideas have influenced parts of the ecology movement. Our relations to technology, consumption and the environment may be driven by unconscious factors.

WHY DO WE LOVE OUR CARS SO MUCH? IS IT JUST BECAUSE THEY ARE USEFUL?

RECENTLY, PSYCHOANALYTIC PSYCHOTHERAPISTS HAVE BEEN CONSULTED IN RELATION TO THE POLITICAL PROCESS.

The effect of social policy on emotional well-being, and the infuence of emotional life on the construction of social policy, may become central to the political agenda.

Paradigm and Theory

Third, psychoanalysis is the paradigm psychotherapy.

AS SUCH, IT IS AN INFLUENCE ON THE BURGEONING FIELD OF COUNSELLING, PSYCHOTHERAPY, SOCIAL WORK AND OTHER PROFESSIONS.

Fourth, psychoanalysis has become a subject of academic study in its own right. There are university courses now devoted to it and it has been applied to many other disciplines. From the study of War to the analysis of Humour (they both contain a lot of aggression); from art, literature, cinema and the theatre, to political leadership or economics.

Can psychoanalysis say anything about the future?

If the future of the individual is partly determined by the past through the continuing influence of unconscious "forces" (wishes, phantasies, unresolved traumas), could it be that the future of our species is similarly determined?

Are we heading blindly toward a future that is determined by the unconscious influences of the past? Can we afford not to think about the irrational forces that propel us?

Further Reading

Bateman, A. and Holmes, J., *Introduction to Psychoanalysis: Contemporary Theory and Practice*, London: Routledge, 1995. A lucid introductory text, written by a psychoanalyst and a psychotherapist, concentrating on clinical practice.

Benvenuto, B. and Kennedy, R., *The Works of Jacques Lacan: An Introduction*, London: Free Association Books, 1986. A comprehensible introduction to Lacan's often difficult writings.

Ekins, R. and Freeman, F. (eds.), *Anna Freud: Selected Writings*, London: Penguin Books, 1998. A representative selection of Anna Freud's work.

Etchegoyan, R.H., *The Fundamentals of Psychoanalytic Technique*, London: Karnac Books, 1998. A massive work of reference sifting through every aspect of analytic technique.

Ferenczi, Sándor, *Selected Writings*, ed. Julia Borossa, London: Penguin Books, 1999. A new translation of Ferenczi's major papers, showing the development of a brilliant analytic thinker.

Freud, S., *The Interpretation of Dreams*, Penguin Freud Library Vol. 4, London: Penguin Books, 1976 (orig. 1900). Freud's first truly "psychoanalytic" book and per-haps, along with *The Origin of Species*, one of the two greatest books ever written.

Freud, S., *Introductory Lectures in Psychoanalysis*, Penguin Freud Library Vol. 1, London: Penguin Books, 1973 (orig. 1917). Some of Freud's most accessible expla-nations of his early theories.

Freud, S., *New Introductory Lectures in Psychoanalysis*, Penguin Freud Library Vol. 2, London: Penguin Books, 1973 (orig. 1931). Some of Freud's most dense and difficult – but fascinating and rewarding – explanations of his later theories.

Hinshelwood, R.D., *A Dictionary of Kleinian Thought*, London: Free Association Books, 1989. The definitive explanation and discussion of major Kleinian concepts.

Klein, Melanie, *The Selected Melanie Klein*, ed. Juliet Mitchell, London: Penguin Books, 1986. A good selection of Klein's essays, introduced by Juliet Mitchell.

Kline, Paul, *Psychology and Freudian Theory*, London and New York: Routledge, 1984. An interrogation of psychoanalytic ideas from the standpoint of psychology.

Rycroft, Charles, *Critical Dictionary of Psychoanalysis*, London: Penguin Books, 1995. Concise and illuminating explanations of psychoanalytic terms.

Sandler, J., Dare, C. and Holder, A., *The Patient and the Analyst*, revised and expanded by Joseph Sandler and Anna Ursula Dreher, London: Karnac Books, 1992 (orig. 1973). Classic text describing the analytic process, recently updated.

Wallerstein, Robert, *The Talking Cures*, New Haven and London: Yale University Press, 1995. Mammoth survey of all the major kinds of psychotherapy.

Winnicott, Donald, *The Child, The Family and the Outside World*, London: Penguin Books, 1991 (orig. 1964). An accessible introduction to Winnicott's thought.

Biographical Notes on Psychoanalysts

Wilfred Bion (1897–1979)
Kleinian psychiatrist and psychoanalyst, who began his career as a reformer of
military psychiatry. Very influential. Made important contributions to questions related
to group psychology, analytic technique and early mother-child interaction.

Christopher Bollas (b. 1943)
Psychoanalyst who has extended Winnicott's work in a number of significant books
including *Forces of Destiny* (1989), *Cracking Up* (1995) and *The Mystery of Things*
(1999). In *Hysteria* (2000) he reaffirmed the significance of Freud's most contentious
sexual theories.

John Bowlby (1907–90)
British psychoanalyst and specialist in child psychiatry. He developed the influential
theory of "Attachment" in the 1950s, and studied the mother-child relation, separation, loss, mourning and depression.

Ronald Fairbairn (1889–1964)
Developed an alternative theory of endopsychic structure to Freud's structural
hypothesis, and investigated the early "persecutory" first stages of life. His
Psychoanalytic Studies of the Personality (1952) describes mental development in
terms of objects-relationships.

Sándor Ferenczi (1873–1933)
Hungarian psychoanalyst, one of Freud's earliest collaborators. Developed theories
of the development of the sense of reality; introjection and transference; and sexual
trauma. Experiments in "mutual analysis" and more focused techniques.

Anna Freud (1895–1982)
Sigmund Freud's daughter, and a pioneer of child analysis. Founded the Hampstead
Clinic (now the Anna Freud Centre), a child therapy institute where she created her
theories of child development, set up research projects and established a training for
child psychoanalysts. Published *Normality and Pathology in Childhood* in 1965.

Edward Glover (1888–1972)
Pioneer of psychoanalysis and one of the most influential figures in the British
Psychoanalytical Society. Wrote polemical works such as *Freud or Jung* (1950), as
well as works on analytic technique, training and the development of the ego.

André Green (b. 1927)
French psychoanalyst who has tried in his writings to synthesize the traditions of
Winnicott, Bion and Lacan. Books include *The Tragic Effect* (1992), *The Work of the
Negative* (1999) and *The Fabric of Affect in the Psychoanalytic Discourse* (1999).

Paula Heimann (1899–1982)
German-born psychoanalyst who emigrated to Britain in 1933. She was a staunch
supporter of Melanie Klein for many years, but surprisingly dissociated herself from
the Kleinian group in 1956. She developed the modern theory of countertransference
and other technical concepts.

Karen Horney (1885–1952)
Born in Hamburg; medical doctor and psychoanalyst, founding member of the Berlin
Psychoanalytic Institute in 1920. Emigrated to the USA in 1932. One of the first neo-
Freudian revisionists, she developed a feminist critique of Freud's views.

Ernest Jones (1879–1958)

First British psychoanalyst and founder member of the International Psychoanalytic Association. Co-founded and edited the *International Journal of Psychoanalysis*. Applied psychoanalytic theory to many topics: literary theory, religion, questions of national identity, anthropology. He dedicated his last years to writing the authoritative biography of Freud, *The Life and Works of Sigmund Freud* (1953-7).

Melanie Klein (1882–1960)

Born in Vienna. Joined the Berlin Psychoanalytic Institute in 1921, and in 1926 moved to London. With the support of Ernest Jones, she became one of the most significant British psychoanalysts. Introduced concepts of the part object ("good" and "bad" breast), the paranoid-schizoid and depressive positions, and projective identification. Her school is now one of the most influential in British psychoanalysis.

Heinz Kohut (1913–81)

Viennese psychoanalyst; emigrated to the USA in 1940. Became training analyst at the University of Chicago. Placed the concept of the "self" at the core of his theories, and became extremely influential through his books *The Analysis of the Self* and *The Restoration of the Self*.

Julia Kristeva (b. 1941)

A practising psychoanalyst who is also a professor of linguistics at the University of Paris VII. She is widely regarded as one of the most significant French thinkers writing today. Books include *Powers of Horror* (1982), *Tales of Love* (1987), *Black Sun: Depression and Melancholia* (1989) and *New Maladies of the Soul* (1995).

Jacques Lacan (1901–81)

Highly influential French psychiatrist and psychoanalyst who reacted against the prevalent American ego psychology in the 1950s. Led a "return to Freud", gaining an international reputation as an original interpreter of Freud's work through his seminars at the University of Paris from 1953. Founded his own school and training.

Margaret Mahler (1897–1985)

Child analyst, noted for her contribution to an understanding of the first years of life through observations and experiments conducted at the Yale University Child Study Center. She introduced the concept of "symbiosis" and wrote, with F. Pine and A. Bergman, the now-classic study *The Psychological Birth of the Human Infant* (1975).

Donald Meltzer (b. 1922)

Trained in medicine and child psychiatry in the USA, but came to England in 1954 to train with Melanie Klein. Has been contributing to Kleinian theory for 35 years in the areas of adult, child and adolescent psychopathology, developmental theory and the training of psychoanalysts.

Juliet Mitchell (b. 1940)

Born in New Zealand; has lived in England since 1944; Freudian psychoanalyst. Wrote *Woman's Estate (*1971), but best known for *Psychoanalysis and Feminism* (1974), which promotes Freudian psychoanalysis as a coherent theory of patriarchy.

Fred Pine (b. 1931)

Psychiatrist and adult psychoanalyst. Worked with Margaret Mahler at Yale and wrote *Developmental Theory and Clinical Process* (1985) and *Drive, Ego, Object and Self* (1990).

Wilhelm Reich (1897–1957)
Psychoanalyst who tried to combine Marxist politics with the advocacy of sexual education and freedom. Developed the important theory of "character armour" and wrote *The Mass Psychology of Fascism* (1933).

John Rickman (1891–1951)
British psychoanalyst and psychiatrist; analysed by Ferenczi and Freud. He wrote about psychoanalysis, psychiatry and medicine, and had an important role in the organization of psychoanalysis in England.

Joseph Sandler (1927–98)
Eminent psychoanalyst, originally from South Africa. Former editor of the *International Journal of Psychoanalysis*. His influential seminars at the Hampstead Clinic analysed basic concepts and developed new psychoanalytic models and theories of clinical practice, which he published in numerous books and papers.

Roy Schafer (b. 1922)
Training and Supervising Analyst at Columbia University. Argued for a hermeneutic understanding of psychoanalysis in *A New Language for Psychoanalysis* (1976) and *Tradition and Change in Psychoanalysis* (1997).

Hanna Segal (b. 1918)
Born in Poland. Influential psychoanalyst in the Kleinian tradition in Britain. Has published works on child analysis, dreams, psychosis, artistic creativity, symbol formation and other topics. Also concerned with the issue of nuclear disarmament.

Donald Spence (b. 1926)
Psychoanalyst and Professor of Psychiatry. Concerned with the scientific status of psychoanalysis in his books *Narrative Truth and Historical Truth* (1982), *The Freudian Metaphor* (1988) and *The Rhetorical Voice of Psychoanalysis* (1994).

James Strachey (1887–1967)
English psychoanalyst, briefly analysed by Freud. He and his wife Alix Strachey devoted their lives to translating and editing the *Standard Edition* of Freud's work. Developed the concept of "mutative interpretation".

Harry Stack Sullivan (1892–1949)
American psychiatrist and psychoanalyst who worked with schizophrenic patients, developed a theory based on interpersonal and social relationships. Elaborated his ideas in *The Interpersonal Theory of Psychiatry* (1953) and other works.

Donald Winnicott (1896–1971)
Paediatrician and psychoanalyst. Prolific contributions to medical, psychiatric and psychoanalytic journals. Wrote in magazines for the general reader and broadcast about children and family problems. Theory of the "good enough mother" and the "transitional object".

Biographical Notes on Psychologists

Wilhelm Wundt (1832–1920) was a prolific writer in many fields who taught the first course in scientific psychology at the University of Heidelberg in 1862. In 1879 he opened the first recognized laboratory for the study of human behaviour in Leipzig.

William James (1842–1910) taught physiology and psychology at Harvard University. In 1890 he published *The Principles of Psychology*. Wrote *The Varieties of Religious Experience* (1902) and developed the philosophy of Pragmatism.

Alfred Binet (1857–1911) played a dominant role in the development of experimental psychology in France. One of the originators of "intelligence tests". In 1895, he opened a Paris laboratory for child study and experimental teaching. His concept of sexual fetishism was discussed by Freud in *Three Essays on the Theory of Sexuality* (1905).

Carl Gustav Jung (1875–1961) coined the term "complex" for emotionally-charged clusters of associations withheld from consciousness. Published *Psychological Types* (1921), in which he proposed the concepts of the extroverted and introverted personality. Developed the concepts of archetypes, persona, individuation, anima and animus, and the collective unconscious, in hundreds of publications until his death in 1961.

Ivan Petrovich Pavlov (1849–1936) developed the concept of the conditioned reflex. In the now-classic experiment, he trained a hungry dog to salivate at the sound of a bell, which was previously associated with the sight of food. He developed a similar conceptual approach in his pioneering studies of human behaviour.

Jean Piaget (1896–1980) developed his "genetic epistemology" of children's thinking from the 1930s. He wrote books dealing with children's conceptions of time, space, physical causality, movement and the world in general.

B.F. Skinner (1904–90) extended behaviourism in the 1930s. Radically criticized "mentalistic" explanations in which behaviour is explained by reference to wishes, thoughts, intentions and so on. Invented the Skinner box.

Hans Eysenck (1916–97) argued that psychotherapy has no proven therapeutic effect, and may be worse than no treatment at all. He devised "behaviour therapy" and developed personality tests from which he derived three fundamental dimensions of personality: extroversion-introversion, neuroticism, and psychoticism.

Acknowledgements

The Author would like to thank Rita Apsan for her picture research and help with the biographical notes, Arnold Brown for his ideas for psychoanalytic cartoons, and Melanie McKennell for her critical reading of early drafts and for putting up with me. I would also like to thank Richard Appignanesi for his work in shaping the text and for general support and encouragement.

The Artist thanks Judy Groves for her creative photographic contribution, Bill Mayblin – the man behind the mask, Marta Rodriguez who also posed for photographs, and finally Erica Davies for allowing us to use the Freud Museum, Alex Bento, Francisco Da Silva for facilitating our photographic sessions, without whose friendly help, my ideas for this book could not have been realized.

Photographs: Judy Groves

Prints: Arabella Anderson
Cover photograph: Arabella Anderson

Index